EX LIBRIS

DARKNESS IS AS LIGHT

Devotions for Persisting in Hard Places

Park End Books
Sugarland

2020

Copyright © 2020 Park End Books.
ALL RIGHTS RESERVED

Cover art & design; illustrations: David Moses
Cover art & illustrations Copyright © David Moses

Publisher's Cataloging-in-Publication Data

Names: Kinard, Summer, 1977- editor.
Title: Darkness is as light : devotions for persisting in hard places / edited by Summer Kinard; illustrations and design by David Moses
Description: Sugarland [Texas] : Park End Books, 2020.
Identifiers: ISBN: 978-1-953427-00-7
Subjects: Religion - Christian Living - Devotional, Religion - Christian Living - Personal Growth
Library of Congress Control Number: 2020917853

All scripture quotations are from Revised Standard Version of the Bible, copyright 1952 [2nd edition, 1971] by the Division of Christian Education of the National Council of the Churches of Christ in the United States of America. Used by permission. All rights reserved.

www.parkendbooks.com

FOR OUR HOLY VIRGIN MARY,

BLESSED AMONG US

CONTENTS

INTRODUCTION – Summer Kinard - vi

SECTION ONE -- PROVISION

- *When the Mother Knew Diogenes Never Watched His Child Convulse* – Allison Boyd Justus - 2
- *Harvest* – Emily Hubbard - 4
- *Need* – A.N. Tallent - 6
- *Humus* – Sarah Lenora Gingrich - 8
- *Provision* – Edith Adhiambo - 10
- *Compassion Cycle* – Christina Baker - 12
- *Literal Actions* – Emry Sunderland - 14
- *Belonging* – Ree Pashley - 16

SECTION TWO -- SWEETNESS

- *Resolute* – Allison Boyd Justus - 20
- *Doves* – Kristina Roth - 22
- *Miracle* – Phoebe Farag Mikhail - 24
- *Here I Am* – Emily Byers - 26
- *A Light Thing in the Sight of the Lord* – Lynnette Ochieng - 28
- *Attired* – Sara Lenora Gingrich - 30
- *Gossip* – Ree Pashley - 32
- *Delayed Message* – Bev Cooke - 34

SECTION THREE -- HEALING

- *Darkness is as Light* – Bev Cooke - 38
- *Run to* – A.N. Tallent - 40
- *Troubled* – Summer Kinard - 42
- *Crying Shame* – Christina Baker - 44
- *Girl: Icon* – A.N. Tallent - 46
- *Arranged* – Bev Cooke - 48
- *Restoration* – Sharon Ruff - 50
- *Lament* – Ree Pashley - 52

SECTION FOUR -- DEATH

- **Miriam's Wilderness Prayer** – Allison Boyd Justus - 56
- **Honey in the Carcass** – Lynnette Ochieng - 58
- **Tea** – A.N. Tallent - 60
- **Turning** – Stasia Braswell - 62
- **Would I Have Missed Him?** – Andrea Bailey - 64
- **The Spirit Gives Live** – A.N. Tallent - 66
- **Comforter** – Emily Hubbard - 68
- **The Shadow of Death** – Beth Thielman - 70

SECTION FIVE -- BALM

- **Cup of Trembling** – Summer Kinard - 74
- **Steady** – Stasia Braswell - 76
- **Trust** – Catherine Hervey - 78
- **Cringe** – Emily Byers - 80
- **Hidden Face** – Laura Wilson - 82
- **Children Within** – Christina Baker - 84
- **Perfect in Weakness** – Edith Adhiambo - 86
- **Light in Darkness** – Laura Wilson - 88

SECTION SIX -- HELP

- **Tamar Twice-Widowed, Accused** – Allison Boyd Justus - 92
- **Disability Life** – Stasia Braswell - 96
- **Like the Leper** – Emily Byers - 98
- **In the Quiet** – Laura Wilson - 100
- **If Anyone; If You** – A.N. Tallent - 102
- **Faithful** – Sarah Lenora Gingrich - 104
- **Sounding** – Andrea Bailey - 106
- **Stealing the Spear** – Summer Kinard - 108

SECTION SEVEN -- TRIAL

- **Shift:Plunge (After Psalm 42)** – Allison Boyd Justus - 112
- **Does He Care?** – Emily Byers - 114
- **Knowing Love** – A.N. Tallent - 116

- *Go Back* – Sharon Ruff - 118
- *Breathless* – Sharon Ruff - 120
- *The Light* – A.N. Tallent - 122
- *The Burning* – Emry Sunderland - 124
- *He Hid Not His Face* – Christina Baker - 126

SECTION EIGHT -- CONSOLATION

- *Platytera* – Nicole M. Roccas - 130
- *Unbroken* – A.N. Tallent - 132
- *Embrace* – Sara Lenora Gingrich - 134
- *Astonishing* – Christina Baker - 136
- *Taken Up* – A.N. Tallent - 138
- *Song* – Summer Kinard - 140
- *Great Is Thy Faithfulness?* – Emily Hubbard - 142
- *Heartbeat* – Stasia Braswell - 144

SECTION NINE -- CLOSER

- *Bath-Jephthah's Wilderness Ride* – Allison Boyd Justus - 148
- *Ordinary Martyrdom* – Monica Spoor - 150
- *Gossamer* – Sarah Lenora Gingrich - 152
- *Goth* – A.N. Tallent - 154
- *Before Dawn* – Stasia Braswell - 156
- *Unashamed* – Edith Adhiambo - 158
- *You Want Me to What?* – A.N. Tallent - 160
- *The Way* – Summer Kinard - 162

ABOUT THE AUTHORS - 165

ABOUT PARK END BOOKS - 172

INTRODUCTION

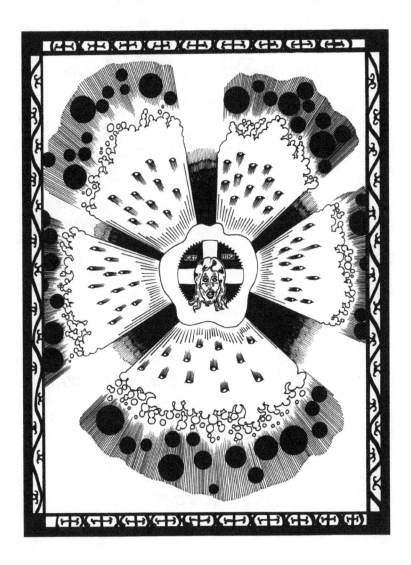

IF YOU CONTINUE IN MY WORD, YOU ARE TRULY MY DISCIPLES, AND YOU WILL KNOW THE TRUTH, AND THE TRUTH WILL MAKE YOU FREE.

JOHN 8:31-32

SO IF THE SON MAKES YOU FREE, YOU WILL BE FREE INDEED.

JOHN 8:36

NOW THE LORD IS THE SPIRIT, AND WHERE THE SPIRIT OF THE LORD IS, THERE IS FREEDOM.

II COR 3:17

FREEDOM THROUGH WITNESS

When I envisioned this devotional, I had two firm images in my heart: the Mother of God standing at the foot of the Cross, and Hagar refusing to look upon the death of her child. They represent the trope in the scriptures between freedom and slavery. The free mother stood at the foot of the Cross, bearing witness even to His death, and the one who had lived in bondage looked away when her son was in danger of perishing. Surely their examples showed the heart of this devotional: bearing witness is the sign of freedom.

Yet I could not settle my mind around this contrast, for Hagar was not in control of her freedom. She had been owned, used, abused, and cast aside. I could not judge her for not bearing witness or read her story as a foil for the heroine Sarah. I could not tidy her away into a typological category. I reached out to our book designer and illustrator, David Moses, with my dilemma. He pointed out what I had missed: the father of nations might have cast Hagar aside, but God Himself comforted her, spoke to her through an angel, and provided water for her and her son in the desert. She must have risen up and borne witness, or we would not have her experience preserved. Abraham had freed her when he cast her out, but it was only after God spoke to her that she was truly free. Suddenly the thesis of this book broadened: God is consistent in mercy despite apparent contrasts and present with us in suffering no matter how we respond to it. We who walk with God find freedom even when we are not free from suffering. The sign of that freedom is bearing witness. More than that, bearing witness to God makes us free.

A GOTHIC DEVOTIONAL

As I write this introduction, I am rejoicing that a relative who was missing has been found. She is safe and, for the moment, sober. When she was lost, I sought out mature Christian women friends to help us pray. I needed my sisters to bear witness with me that God loves the lost ones and calls the spent ones "daughter." When the stakes were high, I was wary of making a general appeal for prayer, because there is a lot of artifice that passes for prayer these days.

Too often, prayer is presented as a tame thing, an accessory to a scripted and tidy life. Too often, the corollary in women's devotions are scrubbed of any hint of danger or vulnerability. They are ornaments for the tamed façade that cannot nurture or heal. They are mere advertisements for a type of marketable womanhood that is foreign to real Christian women's lives. Tamed prayer cannot face suffering, nor can it bear witness to God with us everywhere and in every situation. Tamed faith cannot dispel shame or reach out to reclaim in love a sister gone astray.

But God doesn't require a middle class, photogenic, polished, safe existence before dwelling among us. We who abide in Him and He in us are not called to be pretty or presentable, but to bear much fruit. (Orchards and gardens are messy. So is life.) God doesn't ask of any of us that we not suffer. What I wanted when my relative was lost was a Gothic faith, a pre-Reformation women's faith that was richly reliant upon God and expected God to be with women in suffering. Gothic devotions can reach the lost woman, the too-much woman, the woman who loves and hurts, the woman who grieves and hopes, who desires and disciplines herself to receive God. Gothic faith can reach the woman who doesn't have her life together or a quip to summarize her love; God is enough of a moral to the story.

I put out a call for a Gothic devotional, trusting that the right authors would hear the call and bear witness without pulling their punches, without tidying away their womanhood, their vulnerability, their bravery, or their womb-deep understanding of how God fills all things and redeems suffering with joy if one can wait. Darkness is as Light takes up the themes of the Gothic time period, and it holds out hope for modern "goths" who wear their grief on their sleeves. This book is Gothic in four senses: Like Gothic architecture, it holds around a center and builds transcendence out of heaviness. Like Gothic women's writing, strong contrasts and unexpected beauty yield meaning. Like Gothic artwork, through motion it awakens the senses to the presence of eternity in time by embracing what is unsettled. Like Gothic women mystics, it is unapologetically womanly and embodied, unflinching in the face of hardship, because it knows what women know about God.

GOTHIC ARCHITECTURE

Those tremendous buildings heavier than death draw attention to the light, lift the head in awe, fill the body with song when any music sounds in those great stone ribs. When they were built, the cathedrals we think of as vast graynesses would have been vividly painted, filled with iconography and statues. Immortal angels would have guarded the dead. Flowers and fruit would have blossomed and ripened on stone.

I had prayed in Gothic-style chapels many times, but I understood the power of Gothic architecture for the first time when I visited the great Gothic cathedrals and ruins in England and Scotland. I stood under the high arch in the cathedral next to stones larger than my car and ten times as heavy. All that weight stacked up hard by the empty air drew my eyes up, stone by stone. At the center of the arch was a keystone. It was smaller than most of the other stones, but it held all the heaviness together. With it, there was a cathedral. Without it, ruins. My life, too, would be a ruin without the keystone of Christ's presence, holding together and supporting all of my heavy burdens until they settle around Him and seem light.

GOTHIC WOMEN'S WRITING

Gothic women's writing, like its architecture, is marked with strong contrasts: Justice and Mercy, Pain and Joy, Sweetness and Suffering, Transcendence and Intimacy. As in architecture, these contrasts do not negate one another, but rather rely on each other to give meaning. The medieval women mystics, such as Hildegard von Bingen, Mechthild of Magdeburg, Hadewijch of Antwerp, Marguerite Porete, Teresa of Avila, Catherine of Genoa, and Catherine of Sienna brought together these contrasts in a distinctly feminine spirituality. Ecstasy and submission, pain and joy together mark the experience of birthing for all women, whether one bears children or participates with God in bringing forth spiritual life.

GOTHIC ARTWORK

The artwork in *Darkness is as Light* is inspired by Gothic women's prayers, particularly those of Hildegard von Bingen, whose high-contrast, unsettling illustrations reflect the challenge of comprehending the intersection of eternity and time, and Mechthild of Magdeburg, whose sweet meditations on the wounds of Christ and the synergy of the soul with the Holy Spirit are reflected in the five-petaled rose and the harp. One image was drawn from far earlier in the Christian tradition, in reference to the Martyrdom of St. Perpetua in AD 203. There the saint recounts a vision of a ladder to heaven that was bordered by sharp implements. At the top of the ladder, she was fed a morsel of such sweetness that she could not describe it when she awoke from the vision, still chewing.

GOTHIC WOMANHOOD

This book is womanly through and through, because it is a compilation of the testimonies of women who have met God in their womanly lives. Before the dissolution of Byzantium in the East and the Reformation in the West, women led great centers of spiritual learning, prayer, service, and community. In the United States, monasteries are few and far between, depriving most of us of the insights of spiritual direction by other women. Christian women content creators are in short supply who care for one another spiritually and seek to feed each other as living beings growing into the fullness of Christ. One rarely encounters a book for Christian women that bears witness to Christ with women rather than attempts to tidy and boss them into a socially acceptable (even if spiritually dead) facsimile of an idea about what a Christian woman ought to be. But facsimiles of model women cannot grow into the fullness of God; only real women made in God's image, fully loved by God right where they are, can be saved. Salvation (Theosis) comes to women in the contrasts and complexities of women's lives, not despite them.

Each of the testimonies in this book is offered as encouragement from one woman to another. They do not resolve the tensions that go with receiving God into complicated parts of our lives, but they proclaim God's presence and providence. They demonstrate faith, hope, or love. If you care spiritually for women, these devotionals are a rare gift: spiritual care for women, of women, not at women.

A BAND OF WITNESSES

The women disciples of the Lord went in love to the grave of Christ, carrying sweet spices to what they thought would be the stinking grave. They were stopped by the angel and given a new mission, to go and tell the other disciples what they saw so unexpectedly: Christ is risen. While it was still dark, life dawned from the grave. The women were the ones prepared to see it.

To those of you who walk in darkness, who are struggling through a long night of the soul, a time of grief or trauma or pain, your sisters have offered in these pages to walk with you. We pray that these testimonies will show you that you are not alone. We are the hands reaching sideways to you in your darkness, to bear witness that God is alongside us even when we cannot see. We expect like our foremothers to meet God while it is still dark. We know that God sees you, for to Him darkness is as light.

SUMMER KINARD

Senior Editor, Park End Books
The Nativity of Our Most Holy Lady the Theotokos, 2020

PROVISION

DARKNESS IS AS LIGHT

WHEN THE MOTHER KNEW DIOGENES NEVER WATCHED HIS CHILD CONVULSE

chasing the son of the hounded scoundrel king on the run who starving
scarfed the holy bread of presence down unpunished, she bellowed.

shaken by her ceaseless howl, his friends begged him to chase her off.
he said he'd only come for lost sheep of the god-wrestler.

she heard are you a god-wrestler
and rising answered yes.

he said it isn't good to toss
the children's bread to dogs.

she answered yes and dogs can eat the crumbs;
your children don't eat neatly   and the table's heaped

steaming yeasty loaves of wheat and barley
rise, piled high a surplus of tumbling abundance

yeast cannot stay hidden

after sudden feast
a dozen baskets brimmed

hipparchia's daughter
limp crusty triumph
persist until stones break as bread

Allison Boyd Justus

OTHER SEEDS FELL ON GOOD SOIL AND BROUGHT FORTH GRAIN, SOME A HUNDREDFOLD, SOME SIXTY, SOME THIRTY.

MATTHEW 13:8

HARVEST

I love this verse because I love to garden. There's nothing like the thrill of feeding your family vegetables you've grown yourself. I get such a joy from watching plants come out of seeds, seeing the strength of the life force that God has created. But this year, between the squirrels' eating my tomatoes, mosquitoes' making garden work unbearable, and the derecho bringing branches down on my tomatoes, my harvest is not abundant. Every single vegetable I harvest feels like a triumph. I wouldn't even call the harvest thirty-fold.

Sometimes it seems our Christian world only cares about the hundredfold harvest, whether it's highly visible or small daily acts of faithfulness "that reap a great harvest." Like my sad garden, our hopes for a great harvest can be thwarted by our circumstances. The demands of motherhood and depression derailed both my plans for daily faithfulness and writing bestsellers for Jesus. I saw my friends and peers doing what I want to be doing--writing good books, adding a second income to their family budget, opening their homes to others--but I spent years in a new-baby fog and months barely functioning as a parent and spouse, let alone writing. My harvest was staying alive and loved, and occasionally, ripe tomatoes in September.

This verse shows there's no harvest requirement for you to be good soil. And it's fine for you to be good soil that produces thirtyfold. If you are destroying your life to be super productive for Jesus, or beating yourself up because you haven't converted everyone in your life, please take several deep breaths and remember: thirtyfold is in the Bible. You're still good soil. Jesus is the one who provides the seed, and he knew your harvest before he scattered the seed. Trust and rest in Him.

Emily Hubbard

AS FOR ME, I AM POOR AND NEEDY; BUT THE LORD TAKES THOUGHT FOR ME. THOU ART MY HELP AND MY DELIVERER; DO NOT TARRY, O MY GOD!

PSALM 40:17

NEED

I may live in the United States, but I know what it's like to starve. Not just miss a meal or two; I mean perpetual hunger, going days living off of crackers, my mouth watering at things that had disgusted me before. Both my husband and I worked part-time and were full-time students. Rent for our flea-infested mobile home took up almost half our monthly earnings. Utilities, student loans, and gas took the rest, leaving us with fifty dollars a month for groceries. We didn't have paid time off or sick leave. We couldn't afford healthcare. We worked through any illnesses that came up knowing that a missed day of work would literally take the food out of our mouths.

The day we qualified for food stamps was a godsend. I know what people say about those of us who've been on welfare: "Lazy. Drug addicts. Taking advantage of the system." We were none of those things. We were just hungry, living in a town where graduates and Ph.D.'s jostled to get hired as coffee baristas so they could cater to the few who still had money. We were victims of economic depression and circumstances beyond our control. I'm willing to bet that most welfare recipients are.

Lost at the bottom of the pyramid, God was with us. We felt His care in the random check, the gift from a stranger, the bank account that miraculously still had money even though all our calculations showed otherwise. By God's grace, we survived.

Today, when I fast, I remember the hunger of those days. When I give alms or fill food pantries, I recall the days I emptied them, when twenty dollars was a fortune. Above all, I remember that God loved me, the poor. So, I too, try to love them as myself.

A.N. Tallent

LET THE FAVOR OF THE LORD OUR GOD BE UPON US, AND ESTABLISH THE WORK OF OUR HANDS UPON US, YEA, THE WORK OF OUR HANDS ESTABLISH THOU IT.

PSALM 90:17

HUMUS

I hadn't felt it before, not really. Depression was external to me, it's cold fingers hadn't yet touched my skin, much less my heart. There'd been pain, there'd been darkness, but not the kind that tugged downward from within, like a sinkhole, mercilessly hungry.

We'd come "home" from Chile, where we'd been long-term missionaries, but in truth I felt bereft of home entirely. I loved our life under the shadow of the Andes in Puerto Montt, where we led Bible studies with local teens and our neighbors. Our daily life was suffused with adventure, and I lived with a buzzing sustenance of adrenaline, novelty, and joy. Arriving stateside everything seemed loud, large, and breathtakingly busy. I wasn't ready for the endless choices, the perpetual rush, the way of parceling out time into boxes, rather than living through the flow of it. Why was I even here?

Had God finished writing the good part of our story? Would the rest be some bland, harried life, plagued by numbing American normalcy? The depression remained for a year, but healing came gradually through the work God gave for my hands. We fixed up a decrepit Victorian home. I planted seeds; I heard His narrative among the weeds needing pulled, and in the faces of my neighbors. I left pieces of my sorrow in the soil, hacked in with the edge of my hoe. My soul said to let the pain rot into humus, to feed the growth of new life.

Nearly ten years have passed since our return. I didn't know a story like this could grow here, in plain old Pennsylvania. I didn't know, but I do now, that God too loves a good story, and that He gives all that we need to live it well.

Sarah Lenora Gingrich

THE BLESSING OF THE LORD MAKES RICH, AND

HE ADDS NO SORROW WITH IT.

PROVERBS 10:22

PROVISION

In July, I had no money to pay rent. After losing my job a year ago, I had exhausted my savings and was deep in debt. I had planned to borrow the rent money from my friends, but they were under tight budgets because of the COVID-19 pandemic. When the deadline for payment reached and the housing agency kept on calling me, I almost lost my mind. The flats I stay in are at a prime location, so the landlord is always quick to evict defaulting tenants. When he himself called me a day after the deadline had passed, I knew eviction was an imminent reality.

That night during my meditation, the lights went off in our neighborhood. In that moment of pitch darkness, the Holy Spirit spoke to me saying, "Why do you limit my provision to only money? Don't you think I can make the landlord waive your rent? Money is just one of my many servants of provision. I am the provider, and I can provide in various ways."

A moment later the lights came back, and my spirit went to this verse in Proverbs.

The Holy Spirit is my witness that to this day, I have not got another call, email or reminder from the agency or the landlord about July's rent. When the August rent sheet came, the section for the previous month's balance read 'o'. God paid my Rent!

If I had gotten a loan from my friends, I would have needed to pay it back and added more debts and sorrows. But the blessing of the Lord made me rich without sorrow. Our God is not in the debts business, because it is for freedom that Christ set me free.

Edith Adhiambo

THUS SAYS THE LORD OF HOSTS: "CONSIDER, AND CALL FOR THE MOURNING WOMEN TO COME; SEND FOR THE SKILLFUL WOMEN TO COME."

JEREMIAH 9:17

COMPASSION CYCLE

I have five children: I spend a good part of my day cleaning up messes. Thus I'm fully aware of how hard many of us, myself included, work to avoid mess. Yet so much of life is messy! Especially some of the best parts—birthing, making love, gardening, making mud pies.

Women's bodies are messy, so these, too, we do our best to control and clean up. Heaven forbid we be too smelly, or hairy, or someone notice we have our period. Sometimes I wonder, however, what are we missing when we hide the messiness of life? The whole world works on the beautiful, simple cycle of the Pascal Mystery – life, death, resurrection. Our bodies follow this cycle every month. We suffer the discomfort of PMS, or cramps, or exhaustion. In my case, the hormones make me cry. A lot.

I can't spend a week every month avoiding children's books, radio stories, and my kid's smiles, so I've tried to think differently about my tendency to tears. What if God has given me, and many other women, these tears as a gift? What if we are called, like the women in Jeremiah, or the women Jesus meets as he carries his cross, to mourn with those who mourn? It sounds like a daunting task, but what if God created women—mothers all of us, biologically or otherwise – to do this very caring, comforting, weeping at the foot of the cross, and to do it naturally, easily, (not to say painlessly) every month?

I have to admit, I am more stable emotionally when I am pregnant or nursing than when I am cycling. And as I ride the waves of these constantly changing hormones, I feel the mood swings and sudden onset of tears acutely. But maybe, instead of cursing my body for being so inconvenient, I can start to welcome and bless God's messy gift of tears as an opportunity for deepening compassion.

Christina Baker

FOR I, THE LORD YOUR GOD, HOLD YOUR RIGHT HAND; IT IS I WHO SAY TO YOU, "FEAR NOT, I WILL HELP YOU.

ISAIAH 41:13

LITERAL ACTIONS

You step into a room not much larger than a closet, with three tall walls and no windows. You say goodbye to friends or family with a few hugs and tears. The fourth and final wall is ceremonially bricked up, sealing you in forever. Row by row, as the mortar sets, you prepare inwardly for your new life. The last brick is in place. It's done. There's only a tiny window where food is passed through. Should someone fail to supply you, you'll go without. You could very well die in this ready-tomb. Now what?

The moment of no return in the life of Mother Julian of Norwich used to scare me. I would freeze into a state of inertia and fear, a great shutting-down internally, the very definition of suffering. Mother Julian committed to a prison-like life to experience Christ's suffering as deeply as she could. Her desire to live her faith through literal interpretation is called a "literal action." To understand her, I imitated Mother Julian's literal action in a shelter not much bigger than hers. For four days, I had no food, water, technology, no bathroom or toilet paper or showers, no conversation. Nor any lights to turn on when it got dark. For four days, I had only my commitment to God, myself, and my community.

I felt connected to Mother Julian as soon as I was 'closed in.' There was no time for worry or fear. I had entered the space laden with hundreds of prayers to offer on behalf of my community, town, and the world. I had no difficulty giving up food, but my thirst drove me. It kept me moving, praying, and recommitting to my prayer.

The darkness and lack of conveniences became my freedom. By day two, I understood that Julian wasn't living walled-up in a state of fear: She had her commitment to God. Nothing else matters in the dark. The moment you make the commitment, you relinquish suffering and surrender to a greater faith. That's Sister Julian's secret.

Emry Sunderland

THIS ONE WILL SAY, 'I AM THE LORD'S,'

ANOTHER WILL CALL HIMSELF BY THE NAME

OF JACOB,

AND ANOTHER WILL WRITE ON HIS HAND.

'THE LORD'S,'

AND SURNAME HIMSELF BY THE NAME OF

ISRAEL.

ISAIAH 44:5

BELONGING

This passage inspired me so much that I had "I belong to the Lord" tattooed on the inside of my forearm. It reminded me that it was God who formed me, and God who has promised to help me. When my life is as dry as a desert, God has vowed to cause streams to spring up and trees to flourish. A beautiful thought, right?

Beyond just being a nice idea, God used this verse (and my own tattoo) to save me.

I was in an abusive relationship and thought I shouldn't leave because we were married. One day, I sat down on the couch to cry and begged God for direction. I felt God clearly tell me to look down at my arm – not the arm which was bruised from my husband's angry grip – the other arm. My tattooed arm. And as I looked down at the words inked into my skin, I felt the Holy Spirit speak to me: that despite all the titles I use for my identity – daughter, wife, friend, sister- I am first and foremost God's beloved. Understanding my value in God's eyes was everything and I knew I should be safe above all else. That day, I made a decision to honor my identity as 'the Lord's'. Knowing that I belong to the Lord was the encouragement I needed to make a commitment to my own safety.

God has poured so much water over me since that dry time, that now I am flourishing! I am divorced, but I am healthy and whole and safe. Even when I couldn't see my own worth, God reminded me that above all else, I belong to the Lord. He told me that that identity supersedes everything else.

As we grapple with the difficulties of life, as we cry heartbroken on the bedroom floor, let us remember that we belong to God. Let us put at the front of our minds that he has claimed us as his own. And maybe, even get it as a tattoo.

Ree Pashley

SWEETNESS

RESOLUTE

GOD IS HERE

THEREFORE

(when beauty is the only reason,
reason by beauty
alone)

alabaster carved

(the heart will root,
though beauty is its only light,
thirst its only water, darkness only earth)

ornate, translucent, lustre

(spare no cost, no irresolution)

soft enough
to crumble

(the heart will root and bloom,
and in its blooming truth and mercy fuse)

alabaster flask to crack

(myself would be broken, poured out,
resolute)

releasing rush of fragrant nard

(if I am sudden crushed and poured

let pouring-out yield sweetness)

amber oil streams through shards

(amber light through shattered heart)

alabaster shard, alabaster dust, dissolving

(truth into beauty or beauty to truth or to love –
which is solute, which is solvent,
what solution broken open)

salt of alabaster, salt of dust, of tears
precious oil of nard against the common dust

(dust not unto dust again)

what yielding essence at the root
what dissolution of tears to perfume

(own cascading hair against the weeping)

what solute, what solvent, what solution
of truth and beauty and love
(of spirit and water and blood)

Allison Boyd Justus

LIKE A SWALLOW OR A CRANE I CLAMOR, I MOAN LIKE A DOVE. MY EYES ARE WEARY WITH LOOKING UPWARD. O LORD, I AM OPPRESSED; BE THOU MY SECURITY!

ISAIAH 38:14

DOVES

During the week that my young son and I began moving into our new home, a pair of doves made their nest in the tree outside my bedroom. They began sitting on the eggs before any leaves emerged, in late April. Slowly, leaves began to unfurl and shade the doves. Two bobbling heads came into view. The adults opened their own beaks wide to feed the hatchlings, bowing deep.

The same day that the chicks hatched, my son left for his summer visit with his dad 1,500 miles away.

I often spied on the dove family. Perhaps I was living vicariously through them with my own chick far beyond my own reach.

One evening, a big prairie hailstorm swirled through my region. Its stones were nickel- and quarter-sized; its winds unforgiving. The next morning, I found one of the chicks dead by my back door. It was heavy and large, nearly as big as my fist.

There was still one chick left. By now, leaves fully covered their home. Two nights later, wind gusts up to seventy miles per hour twisted and bent the tree's branches. How could it stand up to that in the shallow, flimsy nest? Even though I couldn't find its body the next morning, I assumed the chick had been blown out and perished.

The doves' consistent, never-stopping efforts seemed to have been all in vain. Powers beyond their control dashed their offspring to the ground. As a single mom, I felt the same way. I labor to build a sturdy nest; it has come together in the middle of many storms. But when my chick isn't with me, so much of that effort and foundation is ignored and openly dashed to the ground. It can feel hopeless.

Several days later, I looked up at the dove nest. A fledgling sat on its edge, watching me. It had survived.

Kristina Roth

THOU HAST KEPT COUNT OF MY TOSSINGS; PUT THOU MY TEARS IN THY BOTTLE! ARE THEY NOT IN THY BOOK?

PSALM 56:8

MIRACLE

We knew this baby was not going to make it. She stopped growing months before she was due. But her heart was still beating, and so we waited, hoping against hope, that she might survive. As the due date drew near, my priest husband took to carrying around the baptismal necessities in his car, to be ready at any moment to baptize her, should this baby girl be born alive.

She was born alive. She was baptized and lived for a few more minutes before she took her last breath. Her parents named her Miracle.

She needed white garments to be buried in. I asked my daughter if she would agree to give away her own baptismal gown from when she was baptized, at about two months old, eight years before. My daughter agreed. The gown was too big. We managed to find something tinier.

So many fellow young moms came to the funeral, aching for our sister and her pain. We held our young children close and tried to keep them quiet.

She and her husband carried out the tiny coffin, after the priests anointed it with the spices used to anoint the relics of the saints. At first I avoided looking at her. Her sobs seemed sacred and personal. Yet her grief was also ours. I tried again to look, to feel with her. Again, I looked away, this time unable to bear it.

Later, she would speak of being comforted by her Miracle, about how she could feel her young daughter praying for her. When my husband headed to Egypt to mourn the loss of his mother, with joy Miracle's mother brought us suitcases full of brand-new baby clothes to send to families in need. There was her daughter, working miracles.

Phoebe Farag Mikhail

AND THEY WERE VERY SORROWFUL, AND BEGAN TO SAY TO HIM ONE AFTER ANOTHER, 'IS IT I, LORD?'

MATTHEW 26:22

HERE I AM

When God calls to Isaiah, the prophet says: "Here am I! Send me" (Isaiah 6:8). Likewise, Samuel answers in obedience: "Speak, for your servant hears" (1 Samuel 3:10). The response of the Apostles, and of Judas Iscariot in particular, when Jesus asserts that one of them will betray him, stands in stark contrast to the prophets' humble readiness. The prophets recognize that God sees them, and they acknowledge the hidden wisdom of his choosing them to carry out his work, in spite of their shortcomings.

The Apostles, on the other hand, and most especially Judas, question Jesus' knowledge of their character. They express doubt, perhaps because they do not really know themselves, or perhaps because they do know themselves and are ashamed of their own frailty. They startle like guilty men. They do not want to be truly seen, like Adam hiding in Eden after the Fall.

How absurd, to think we can hide anything from the God who sees everything, but this is what I do every time I put on a false face in prayer. Sometimes I'm trying to obscure my guilt. I multiply my words and intensify my piety, thinking that maybe, if I pray really well, the Lord won't notice those pesky sins I've swept under the rug. In other moments, I wrestle with the realization that God is asking me to do something that scares me, and I respond with false humility. In my early twenties, I was struggling to come to terms with my call to consecrated life. Part of me knew that I had a religious vocation, but that didn't stop me from questioning God's wisdom in choosing me. I told him I was too ordinary, too undisciplined, inadequate to the task – instead of simply asking him to deliver me from my pride.

The Lord can only heal what I reveal to him. If I can't be as humble as the prophets, I can at least acknowledge that he sees me, in spite of my foolish attempts to hide.

Here I am, Lord. Heal me.

Emily Byers

THIS IS A LIGHT THING IN THE SIGHT OF THE LORD; HE WILL ALSO GIVE THE MOABITES INTO YOUR HANDS.

2ND KINGS 3:18

A LIGHT THING IN THE SIGHT OF THE LORD

There is nothing that our Almighty God cannot do. I realized this as I quietly sobbed in my hospital bed, so happy, so grateful to God for a successful surgery and for giving me the privilege of carrying my baby to term and making me a mother.

"Ma'am? Do you have anyone who can sign the theater consent paper for you?" were all the last words I vaguely heard in the labor ward, after I had dilated six centimeters while looking forward to having my first born (a 2.84kg healthy baby boy).

Yet here I was lying in the acute room, after spending close to ten hours in the surgical theater. I had had an anterior uterine rapture that changed everything in blink of an eye. An emergency operation had to be carried out on me. My body had gotten cold and my blood pressure had sunk very low. I could hardly pray. Have you had such moments when you get into some tight situations and just can't pray? Maybe some of you understand me. I was at that point. It is at that point that a small little voice spoke to me saying "Baby, hang in there, this is a little matter before my eyes." And suddenly this scripture II Kings 3:18 flashed over my memory. I felt so much peace within me, and the pain just vanished! Then I smiled.

God was right in the storm. My Daddy was right there, all the while, with me. God never leaves His people. He is always right there. Whatever it is you may be going through, don't give up: It is a light thing in the sight of the Lord! He will handle it!!

Lynnette Ochieng

I WILL GREATLY REJOICE IN THE LORD, MY SOUL SHALL EXULT IN MY GOD; FOR HE HAS CLOTHED ME WITH THE GARMENTS OF SALVATION, HE HAS COVERED ME WITH THE ROBE OF RIGHTEOUSNESS...

ISAIAH 61:10

ATTIRED

It was a late 1980's dream of a dress. Bold graphic print with splashes of neon on white knit, with a front zipper from the hem line up to the neck. My mom excitedly brought it home from a garage sale, and it looked like something my Barbie would wear for a night on the pink town. For a girl who lived in t-shirts and sweatpants, it seemed like an initiation into the mysterious world of fashion.

I dared to zip myself into it; I felt a small thrill of joy at my reflection. I wasn't going to be stylish every day; I too dearly loved tearing around on my bike and climbing trees for that, but I could be sometimes.

It was at recess that a wealthy girl from my neighborhood strode up to me, flanked by her friends. "Nice dress..." she said, with a sneer, "...it was in fashion last year. Your mom bought it at our yard sale." She laughed at me; her friends laughed. It hadn't occurred to me that secondhand clothing was shameful, but my burning face and sinking stomach felt that certainty descend quite forcefully. I ran from them, and I never wore it again.

I wish I'd had my more stalwart heart back then; I would have worn the dress with joy, not caring what anyone thought. But I had a nine-year-old heart, and I did not know my Lord and His boundless joy; not yet. I had no idea of the particular delight He takes in each of His children growing into themselves.

I began to heal in my teens. I showed up to school with bare feet and grass braided into my waist-length hair. God was attiring me with joy, resilience, and authenticity, and it looked good on me.

Sarah Lenora Gingrich

JACOB'S WELL WAS THERE, AND SO JESUS, WEARIED AS HE WAS WITH HIS JOURNEY, SAT DOWN BESIDE THE WELL. IT WAS ABOUT THE SIXTH HOUR. THERE CAME A WOMAN OF SAMARIA TO DRAW WATER. JESUS SAID TO HER, "GIVE ME A DRINK."

JOHN 4:6-7

GOSSIP

When I lived in a remote area of Uganda, I had to carry water three, four times a day from a community water source. It was generally the work of women and girls, and there was a distinct social aspect to it. At the water pump, women shared gossip, girls discussed class assignments, and friendships were forged. We fetched water in the early mornings and evenings. No one collected water at noon.

Given my experience in East Africa, I imagine how ostracized St. Photine, the woman at the well, must have felt. She would have been incredibly lonely drawing water at the time of day when she was guaranteed to not see another woman. Perhaps it was the only way to avoid gossip, but it was also a surefire method to be alone.

Not long after my time in Uganda, I moved to a new location and became the center of false gossip. Already new and trying to make friends, I felt even more isolated by the rumors. I didn't know how to go about addressing the accusations. I felt ostracized and ignored, and in turn, I avoided people. I spent a lot of time crying and journaling. Journaling transitioned to writing out lengthy prayers and meditating on the red-letter words of Christ.

The heart-to-heart between Jesus and St. Photine stands out as Jesus' longest one-on-one conversation recorded in the Gospels. The fact that it occurred with a woman—of ill repute and probably lonely—is significant to me because the gossip around St. Photine was not the focus of the conversation. Jesus connected with her on another level: he revealed himself as the Messiah!

Being the subject of gossip was painful, but Christ offered me a real relationship that broke through my loneliness. Those journaling prayers were the living water that deepened my relationship with the Messiah. Christ reached through my loneliness and met me when I was avoiding interaction.

Ree Pashley

THIS IS WHY I SPEAK TO THEM IN PARABLES, BECAUSE SEEING, THEY DO NOT SEE, AND HEARING THEY DO NOT HEAR, NOR DO THEY UNDERSTAND.

MATTHEW 13:13

DELAYED MESSAGE

"All she wants is to start again when we move out there in June." Dad's voice came through the phone that October evening, he in Toronto with Mum; me on the west coast. "She wants to know if you're willing to try." He said more, and I heard it, but paid little attention, because my heart was soaring! My mother wanted to repair our relationship. Even at thirty-two, I wanted nothing more than for my mother to love me. Maybe now, finally, I was a good enough girl to deserve her love, but she died that December, before we could speak again.

Thirty years later, after a tumultuous healing experience, I confided in my priest about it, seeking confirmation of my experience. He agreed it was real, and then said, "You have to forgive your mother for what she did." I replied I had, years ago, and recounted that long ago conversation. "And she said, then, that the biggest disappointment of her life was that she replicated her and her mother's relationship with me." I stopped dead as I actually heard the words had relayed to me all those years ago. It had taken a while, but I finally had the ears to hear, and the eyes to see. If her relationship with me was the biggest disappointment of her life, that meant that I was the most important thing in her life. And if I was the most important thing in her life, then she must have loved me. She tried to do the best she could, but she didn't know how – all she'd learned about being a mum was how to hurt, because that what was done to her. But she hated that she had hurt the daughter she'd loved more than anyone else. My mother loved me.

Bev Cooke

HEALING

DARKNESS IS AS LIGHT

If I say, "Surely the darkness shall cover me, and the light around me become night," even the darkness is not dark to you; the night is as bright as the day, for darkness is as light to you. (Psalm 139:11-12)

It feels like empty, weary home
When through the hills I pass.
Return to overcast, perpetual night
Dark on dark, black soul, black sky,
That place beyond the hills recedes in mind
to sepia shades and tinny, ghostly voices.
Laughter becomes a forgotten tongue,
A memory of language once mastered, now lost.

Words fall strengthless against the hills,
Thin and insubstantial as the mist,
words of love and gestures of concern
Heard and glimpsed from distances too vast to bridge
Attenuated, love becomes pale friendship,
Friendship wanes to mere acquaintance.
Black night, black hills obscure
fond faces, receding in the dark.

I move through habit, automaton in flesh
Daily round is done by rote – dishes, meals, shopping
covered in dark ash, the prayers mumbled and fumbled,
the printed words penetrate my eyes until I see:
"even the darkness is not dark to you;
the night is as bright as the day,
for darkness is as light to you."
The clouds begin to break, the ash covered hills shrink as the sun
promises to return.

Bev Cooke

HE WHO EATS MY FLESH AND DRINKS MY

BLOOD ABIDES IN ME, AND I IN HIM.

JOHN 6:56

RUN TO

It was the worst summer of my life. I had rushed one thousand miles away from home to tend to my father who lay intubated in ICU after a near-fatal car accident. Every morning I woke up to check work emails before rushing to the hospital, praying Dad would finally breathe on his own while also worrying over his bills, hiring lawyers, talking with doctors, and juggling the inevitable family drama, all while suffering from first trimester nausea. I woke up as tired as when I went to bed with the burning, sterile smell of the hospital following me everywhere I went. It was pure misery.

When I finally made it to a church, I only wanted one thing: the Eucharist. I had just started attending an Anglican church which opened my eyes to the reality of Christ's presence in the bread and wine. It is not mere symbol or allegory. He is truly there, and when I finally recognized that, I felt myself change. The Eucharist – Christ – began to change me. And now, in my utter despair and weakness, there was nothing that could help me but Him. No eloquent sermon, no harmonious music, no smiling face, it was all meaningless against my pain. Only the Eucharist could give me the strength to face what I had to face, to walk into that hospital, to nurture my unborn child, to even get out of bed just one more day.

I've often struggled with the proper way to approach the chalice. Too often we think we must have it all together to take in the body and blood of Christ, but that summer taught me differently. When we are our weakest and worst, the only proper response is to run to the chalice. Run to Christ.

A.N. Tallent

FOR AN ANGEL OF THE LORD WENT DOWN AT CERTAIN SEASONS INTO THE POOL, AND TROUBLED THE WATER: WHOEVER STEPPED IN FIRST AFTER THE TROUBLING OF THE WATER WAS HEALED OF WHATEVER DISEASE HE HAD.

JOHN 5:4

TROUBLED

On my tenth night of Covid-19, I knew that I would either die that night or recover. I stayed awake most of the night, lying on my stomach, making myself pump the heavy bellows of my breath with all my will to live and all my years of disciplined strength from singing. The gravity of my mortality circled the pull of death. I knew my efforts might not be enough. I confessed my sins to God and a favorite saint, in case I never got another chance to go to confession. Near dawn, I felt my breathing ease as though someone had removed a brick from my chest. I closed my eyes in weary relief. When I opened them, I was looking up at the world as though through water. God had troubled the water, and I was in it.

The bricks fell off my chest over the ensuing weeks, but they took my strength with them when they fell. I was left in ruins like a great cathedral, fragments of my former strength standing vulnerable in the wind. My breath goes through me, but I can no longer catch it. After many months, I can breathe and even sing now without pain. My body is rebuilding, but my blood is slow, my brain battered, my stores totally depleted. How many generations worked to give my body its former strength? How long does it take to restore a cathedral?

I cannot lift a shovel to garden. I have to rest between readings to let my brain heal. I can scarcely write without shaking. Every exertion crashes me back down to the bed, to my belly and headache, intentional breathing, exhaustion. I am crashing back under those healing waters, those troubled waters. It's slow, long, weary work, but I will take the trouble to be healed.

Summer Kinard

LET US THEN WITH CONFIDENCE DRAW NEAR TO THE THRONE OF GRACE, THAT WE MAY RECEIVE MERCY AND FIND GRACE TO HELP IN TIME OF NEED.

HEBREWS 4:16

CRYING SHAME

She brought up the end of the communion line, this woman with her wailing child. She had him pinned, one arm under his bottom, controlling the flailing legs, the other hand holding his head to her shoulder. We had been able to hear his distress through the glass window of the cry room, but the sound of his screams dominated the little church as she strode up the aisle. She approached the priest, received the host on her tongue, and turned, retreating to the back of the church again.

The howling didn't pause for a moment.

Her face was set; there was a look in her eyes, behind the thick, brown-framed glasses, that I struggled to name. Resignation? No. Embarrassment? Perhaps. That is what I expected. But more than that, I saw defiance, determination. Nothing, not even a one-year-old screaming like he had been scalded, was going to keep her from receiving Jesus. She was going to meet Him, and she would drag her difficulties along, kicking and screaming, if need be.

My eyes were full of tears as the priest cleaned the sacred vessels and we waited for the closing prayer. I am so easily embarrassed, so fearful of what others might think. Would I have made the trek up the aisle, knowing how many eyes were on me? Or would I have stayed in the cry room, wallowing in frustration and disappointment?

I've been stared down enough times for my own noisy infants to know the feeling of all those eyes quite well. Just as I want to keep my screaming child in the cry room, I'm often tempted to hide my shame and sinfulness – even from God, who wants to hold me in all my shame and pain. The memory of that brave, beautiful mother reminds me to have courage to seek God's face, and to drag with me whatever threatens to keep me from him, and lay that at his feet.

Christina Baker

SO GOD CREATED MAN IN HIS OWN IMAGE, IN THE IMAGE [ICON] OF GOD HE CREATED HIM; MALE AND FEMALE HE CREATED THEM.

GENESIS 1: 27

GIRL: ICON

The ritual went like this: I come home from school and head straight to my bedroom. Don't want to see Mom. Don't want to talk to anyone. Just let me be invisible. Once the door is safely shut and backpack stowed, I turn on my music, lie on the floor, close my eyes, and sink my nails into my own skin. Just a little scratch at first. Then deeper, harder, faster until it starts to burn and tingle and fill my body with nothing but the cool sensation of pain. If I was lucky, I'd even draw blood. I never used a knife, wasn't aiming to kill myself. I just wanted to feel.

My mother was a deeply abusive and mentally unstable narcissist who never missed a moment to imply that my family would be better off without me. To keep her image of perfection, she projected all her hatred onto me and taught my siblings to do the same. My clinically depressed dad was too absorbed in his own battles to notice my hurt. Any hint of rebellion, any sign of emotion, and there was the whole crew of family members eager to silence me into submission. And every day that hatred etched itself onto the arms of a little girl who had no other outlet but to continue in the strain of destruction, believing the lie that she was worthless.

I often wonder how things might have changed for that girl if she was told she was an icon of Christ Who shares in the flesh she's mutilating. I still have trouble believing it. Those golden icons on the walls of the church are so beautiful. Is that how God sees me: valuable, beautiful, worthy of a kiss? Why, then, couldn't my own mother see me that way?

A.N. Tallent

YOU HAVE RAVISHED MY HEART, MY SISTER, MY BRIDE, YOU HAVE RAVISHED MY HEART WITH A GLANCE OF YOUR EYES.

SONG OF SOLOMON 4:9

ARRANGED

My mother gave me fifteen minutes to decide what to do. I was seventeen. In the subtle, wordless ways I had learned early in life, I understood that she wanted me to have an abortion. "We'll never talk about it again," she said afterward. We didn't. I spent far too long drinking too much, hating too much, lashing out too much in an effort to pretend it never happened.

Forty years later, I struggled to write an Akathist to St. Mary of Egypt, using as my themes the Song of Solomon, Peter's walking on the water, the Samaritan woman at the well, and looking for love in all the wrong places. One day, I incorporated part of the above verse into the prayers I wrote. That evening, I went to church see a friend talk about her book about miscarried and still born children. Two icons greeted me in the narthex: St. Peter walking on water, and the woman at the well. The lesson was the Song of Solomon, beginning at the very verse I had included in the Akathist that day. I felt punched in the gut, blindsided, as all of the elements of prayer came together to make a space for me to mourn the loss of my aborted child.

At the panikhida (prayers for the departed) after Vespers, struggling to control myself, I prayed for James, my dead son. I felt him standing on my left, and like a cool sterile lance into a hot, infected wound, his forgiveness flowed over and into me. Joyful tears came freely. How could I be sad any more, when an invisible guilt that had weighed me down was washed away, and I was bathed in a healing balm? I could feel his goodbye kiss on my cheek, as soft as the drip of the anointing oil at my chrismation, and I could almost hear St. Mary of Egypt giggling with joy for arranging all this.

Bev Cooke

HE HEALS THE BROKENHEARTED AND BINDS UP THEIR WOUNDS.

PSALM 147:3

RESTORATION

More than a decade after my husband died, I still felt broken down after the years of caregiving and stress. But one day God showed me a beautiful vision of His restoration power that profoundly changed my perspective. First, He put His hands on my face, gently tipped my head down and kissed me on the forehead. Then He pressed His forehead against mine and began untangling the complicated mess of traumatic memories. Next, He put His hands on my shoulders and felt that every bone was broken in my body from decades of carrying the heavy weight of people, memories, and events.

The bones came back together – bone to bone. As every weight was lifted from me, my frame came into alignment. He located my fractured heart that was well hidden behind high walls of self-protection and replaced the walls with massive windows. Then He invited me to bring Him my bloody and tear-stained garments as a precious memorial of the battles I endured. He assured me that He was not ashamed of me in any way.

He knelt before me, removed my battered shoes, and wept as He gently held my twisted feet in His hands. My feet softened like warm wax, and He reshaped them for my next journey. From there He invited me to rest in His arms as He gently lowered me into the waters to wash my wounds. He told me when He lifted me up, I would be clothed with new garments for the next season of my life. He put beautiful new shoes on my feet and spoke lovingly.

"Oh little one, I know how much this journey has cost you. Now follow me. I delight in you."

Sharon Ruff

IN THE DAY OF MY TROUBLE I SEEK THE LORD;

IN THE NIGHT MY HAND IS STRETCHED OUT

WITHOUT WEARYING;

MY SOUL REFUSES TO BE COMFORTED.

WHAT GOD IS GREAT LIKE OUR GOD? THOU

ART THE GOD WHO WORKEST WONDERS.

PSALM 77: 2, 13-14

LAMENT

When I was going through a painful divorce, I had two friends who wanted to offer support in very different ways. One wanted me to just look on the bright side of everything and would interject advice and suggestions whenever I was sharing my broken heart. Well-intentioned? Certainly. Helpful? Absolutely not.

I needed to cry. It was important for me to grieve the loss of my marriage before going forward.

My other friend was a certified counselor, and she simply listened to me. She gave me tissues when I cried, and she offered me hugs and a cup of tea. Through processing my grief, not simply rushing through it, I was able to acknowledge both the losses and blessings in my life. While I accepted the loss of my marriage and said a final goodbye to my ex-husband, my friend reminded me that she, my family, and my church hadn't gone anywhere. They wanted to support me. I could sob because I was getting divorced and be thankful for my friend who helped me pack and move out.

It was not a time for rejoicing: divorce has an air of mourning about it. But in that black-cloaked time, I could also cherish the good things in my life: a supportive family, loving friends, and of course, the unchanging love of God.

Like the psalm, my own song has a black period of deep sadness; I won't try to fluff it over or pretend everything was okay – it wasn't. Amidst my grief, I also recognized God's blessings in my life. The two are not mutually exclusive: I can be broken-hearted and thankful. My sadness does not mean I have forgotten all that God has done for me. My weeping, as well as my thanksgiving, were both important aspects for my healing. David's words in this lamenting psalm acknowledge suffering. He sits in darkness for a little while, like an empathetic friend who listens until I can give thanks again.

Ree Pashley

DEATH

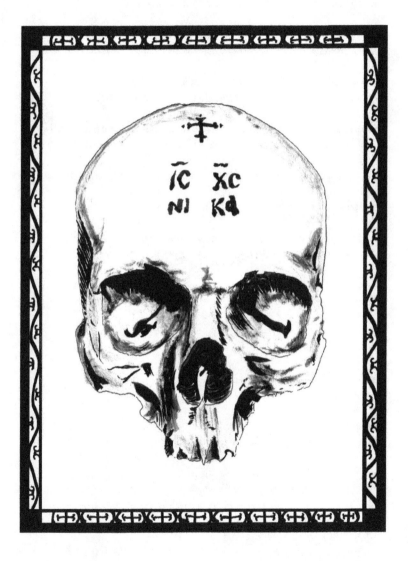

MIRIAM'S WILDERNESS PRAYER

You have removed me from all I know In silence I remember

when you made me prophesy God why strike me now

I remember the narrowness that stalked us to the edge of the sea
My brothers and I did not speak to one another of the mouth of freedom

mouth full of teeth or weigh risk of misdirection: A prison
behind, locked, no re-entry, starlit abyss of unknowing ahead,

Or else aside, clear-eyed into a lie We did not speak to one another of what
could consume us: fear   or fire   spirit incandescent   flood

Each of us silently   apprehended   depths mighty to swallow us   sea-reeds rush
armed chariots rumble, roar deep calls to deep

And now I sorrow, but   I do not know   how to heal or repent I see
you have made my brothers intercede for me You hem me in

before and behind and lay your hand upon me   The people wait
(Do you make   the people wait?)   while you rescue, recreate me

A narrow wind, a new strait
A silence

You breathe dance as prophecy
The sea splits

I sing the narrowness that chased us now has drowned
I sing the prison now cannot be found

In the face of death choose life I sing
What abyss of freedom now will swallow me

What expanse, what fire, what ocean,
what depth, what infinity?

Allison Boyd Justus

HE SCRAPED IT OUT INTO HIS HANDS, AND WENT ON, EATING AS HE WENT; AND HE CAME TO HIS FATHER AND MOTHER, AND GAVE SOME TO THEM, AND THEY ATE. BUT HE DID NOT TELL THEM THAT HE HAD TAKEN THE HONEY FROM THE CARCASS OF THE LION.

JUDGES 14:9

HONEY IN THE CARCASS

It was hardly three months after my baby was laid to rest. The pain from the loss was too much. The healing process was too much. One chilly morning I had woken up and as usual was going through his clothes, all of which I had total held on to. A thought came to me that I could actually find other women who are yet to deliver and gift them with all these new items which my baby never used. I set the thought aside, because I was not ready to set aside the clothes. One day just after my morning devotion, a friend called me and asked if I could begin selling baby clothes to expectant mothers and those with newborn babies. This seemed like a tough call as it could constantly remind me of my baby. I felt like she was trying to torture or mock me, hence I declined!

Fast forward to today: I own a baby shop, selling beautiful clothes to expectant mothers, giving them advice on dressing their babies and taking care of them. I also serve mothers with new born babies. Helping clothe other babies has given me so much joy and peace. I found honey in my carcass.

If you have a mandate from God, the devil will continuously fight you. Samson had a mandate from God.

Friend, some of these challenges we face, only come to make us strong and help us realize the hidden potentials in us. Samson found honey in the carcass. Keep your focus on God. In that carcass, you will find honey to lick! Honey to feed everyone!

Lynnette Ochieng

FOR TRULY, I SAY TO YOU, WHOEVER GIVES YOU A CUP OF WATER TO DRINK BECAUSE YOU BEAR THE NAME OF CHRIST, WILL BY NO MEANS LOSE HIS REWARD.

MARK 9:41

TEA

In October 2011, I found myself in Iwate, Japan, staring at a wasteland. The "Triple Disaster" of earthquake/tsunami/nuclear meltdown had happened just months earlier, devastating the entire northern coast of the country and killing thousands. I walked by ghost towns, buildings reduced to skeletons, cars piled up into mountains of twisted metal, trees stripped of bark and dying from the intake of salt water, and massive steam ships in the middle of the street. I was there as part of a relief team, but what relief could I possibly give to the people who had survived this?

Those survivors still lived in tiny tin boxes, awaiting rebuilding help that was long in coming. They had lost everything and not just material goods. I met a woman who was the lone survivor of her family. I talked with the elderly, born and raised in a community that was instantly washed away by the waves. I gave them blankets and served them tea. It felt like such a paltry gift.

One day, a man came up to our team. "The Buddhist priest told me that this disaster is proof that the gods and Buddha have no control over nature." He said, dissatisfied. "But, I see God when I look at you." We had never even mentioned the name of Jesus, but it didn't matter. To this man, the cup of tea that warmed his hands and heart had been given in His name. And, somehow, he felt that.

Our world is obsessed with the big gestures, the grand displays of charity. I often despair that I'm not doing enough, can never do enough. What, after all, is a cup of water even if it's for Christ? It is such a small thing, but for some, it is a taste of heaven.

A.N. Tallent

AND NOW, O LORD, I HAVE TURNED MY EYES AND MY FACE TOWARDS THEE.

TOBIT 3:12

TURNING

The grave does not always stink of rotting flesh. In some cases, the Deceiver masks it with a fragrance sweeter than honey. I remember a time when I could think of nothing but suicide. Death was so seductive: it promised an embrace of finality and the end of my suffering.

But even when I was under the spell of the grave, I knew that someone would find me. I made myself imagine the consequences if I went through with it: My mother would try to force air into my lifeless body and inevitably fail. She would blame herself for my final choice.

Like Sarah who rejected the option of suicide in the story of Tobit, I could not descend into the grave knowing that I abandoned the people I loved.

I remember the night that I approached the Lord, in literal fear and trembling. I was weeping on my knees in the shower, scalding my body with too-hot water, as if pain could cleanse me. "God," I said, "I am so tired. I need you to make things better or I need you to kill me."

And just as God delivered Sarah, He delivered me in a way and in a fullness that I could have never imagined. I was brought to the Church, which is a blessing beyond comprehension; it is the pearl of great price. I met friends and professionals who have helped me heal. The road is long, and it has taken over a decade to even begin ascending out of the valley of the shadow of death. I still feel the call of grave, urgent and beguiling. Sometimes, all I can do is cry and remember my prayer. I feel drenched in fear and grief.

I am so afraid of the future. I worry that I will find myself in the pits of hell again. I know that suffering is for salvation, but I am so afraid of it. I turn my face toward prayer. I hope it is enough.

Stasia Braswell

AND THE KING WILL ANSWER THEM, "TRULY, I SAY TO YOU, AS YOU DID IT TO ONE OF THE LEAST OF THESE MY BRETHREN, YOU DID IT TO ME."

MATTHEW 25:40

WOULD I HAVE MISSED HIM?

A couple of years ago we moved from a wooded cul-de-sac to an urban setting, fractured by segregation, violence and noise. The tree-lined boulevard we now call home was once one of the finest neighborhoods in this part of the city.

For several blocks, the majestic canopy of trees and stately architecture lull one into sweet reverie and demand admiration; their nature protests the disorder that surrounds us. The residents of this boulevard are the custodians of its regal contours and vigilantly keep watch, allowing the children to play, the yards to blossom and the birds to nest.

But even in their watchfulness, brokenness finds its way in: High speed chases, trash-lined streets, deafening noise, and multiple shootings. It's the kind of violence that undoes the soul, causes sleepless nights and evokes hopeless tears for the landscape before me.

It is easy for me to doubt God's presence in this seemingly forgotten place. Yet it is here that Christ beckons me to see Him – in the homeless man knocking on our door asking to rake our leaves or the woman limping down the street, telling me about her sister's baby, dead in a dumpster.

I have tried to offer what comforts I have. But there is no happy ending to these stories I keep – at least not yet. For now, I am given the chance to bring small comforts to my Lord, mysteriously present in those He brings to my door. For now, I am confronting my own disordered loves, asking God for His help. Would I have missed Him had He not appeared so clearly in the ones before me? God, help me to see while there is still time. Help me to remember you, dwelling in those whom the world has forgotten.

Andrea Bailey

IF THE SPIRIT OF HIM WHO RAISED JESUS FROM THE DEAD DWELLS IN YOU, HE WHO RAISED CHRIST JESUS FROM THE DEAD WILL GIVE LIFE TO YOUR MORTAL BODIES ALSO THROUGH HIS SPIRIT WHICH DWELLS IN YOU.

ROMANS 8:11

THE SPIRIT GIVES LIFE

I was a teenager when I stumbled into the occult. A group of friends joined me in exploring the "spiritual realm" through astral projection, spirit possession, and engaging in what we believed to be worlds unseen. I found myself most drawn to fortune telling. Reading the future in cards or stones and opening myself to the spirits around me so as to get a glimpse of "the beyond" fascinated me. Maybe none of it was real. Perhaps the futures I saw were, in fact, self-fulfilling prophecies. Perhaps the spirits I thought I knew were only the result of an overactive imagination. Regardless, I do not doubt that the devil had his hand on me. The proof was all too evident.

In exchange for my "power," I found myself slowly weakening. I couldn't eat, and my body began to waste away. I became prone to fainting fits and an altogether unstable, anxious mind, scared of what could lurk around every corner. I thought myself better than everyone around me, but inside I was writhing as physical weakness and emotional despair sapped at my life. I wanted to die.

Though I professed to be a Christian, it was obvious that I had traded the Spirit of Life for one of death. Death reigned in my mind and my flesh. Though the devil gives great power to those who want it, there is one thing he cannot do: give life. Only the Holy Spirit can do that, and until I finally surrendered my devil-tainted power, my life was only a shell. I learned a valuable lesson during those years: the spirits of evil are real and they promise much, but to let them into you is to kill one's body and soul. True power – true Life – is the Holy Spirit's alone.

A.N. Tallent

BLESSED BE THE GOD AND FATHER OF OUR LORD JESUS CHRIST, THE FATHER OF MERCIES AND GOD OF ALL COMFORT, WHO COMFORTS US IN ALL OUR AFFLICTION, SO THAT WE MAY BE ABLE TO COMFORT THOSE WHO ARE IN ANY AFFLICTION, WITH THE COMFORT WITH WHICH WE OURSELVES ARE COMFORTED BY GOD.

II CORINTHIANS 1:3-4

COMFORTER

I'll be honest, sometimes these verses give me the warm fuzzies, and sometimes, they make me want to run away. Some days, I would like to trade my abundant comfort for fewer troubles. I want to put my shields up, to keep my painful places held close and safe. I want an abundant life that is more about tasty meals on a screened-in porch, and less an abundance of both comfort and suffering. But I know I can't.

Living in a fallen world means that people will hurt us and our bodies will fail us. Our struggles and troubles are not ours alone. Our unique experiences will still parallel those of others. We will always need comfort and to give comfort.

I was twenty-three when I had my first miscarriage, in our first year of marriage. More than a dozen years later, my heart still twinges thinking about that sad time. I am a stress smoker (sorry), and use those times with a cigarette to talk to Jesus about my feelings. My husband thought that smoking was disgusting, but when I sat on our back step to smoke and mourn after my D&C, he lit one and sat with me. He was a comfort.

Because we put our miscarriage on the church prayer list, many ladies in the church took the time to share their pregnancy and infant loss stories with me. I'm not sure if my openness comforted them or they comforted me, but I know it was better than silence.

I've had two more miscarriages since (and four kids) and though each one was different, I remain comforted by knowing that like my husband was with me, Jesus is with me, and my lost babies are with Him. And when I share the comfort through loss I've been given, even when it hurts, I allow other parents to realize that God's comfort is there for them.

Emily Hubbard

EVEN THOUGH I WALK THROUGH THE VALLEY OF THE SHADOW OF DEATH, I FEAR NO EVIL; FOR THOU ART WITH ME; THY ROD AND THY STAFF, THEY COMFORT ME.

PSALM 23:4

DARKNESS IS AS LIGHT

THE SHADOW OF DEATH

My friend was not supposed to die so young. She was supposed to come home from the hospital; better, alive, ready to see me and laugh with me again.

On my living room floor that sunny April afternoon, I was changed. My hands shaking, my face soaked with tears and mucus, my eyes bloodshot, I was no longer an uncomplicated person. Since then, she has been part of every other loss I have grieved, because she is no longer there to comfort me and to help me through it. Her death, and the loneliness it left in its wake, follows me still. Like a shadow beneath my face, my hands, my body, the darkness of being without a beloved friend lingers.

Since that first darkness, the shadows have lengthened. Two more friends, an aunt, and a father; all went within three years. Each of them casts a shadow of their own. When I was a child, the Valley of the Shadow of Death was a ghoulish place. It was something I hoped to outsmart, to keep behind locked doors. But grief is not a monster. Loss cannot be stuffed into a closet or under a bed.

The Shadow of Death stays with us because it is joined to us. Rather than a foe we must conquer, it is a companion we must meet. It is a fearsome truth we must face. Though I feel alone in the Valley, the Good Shepherd goes ahead of me. He is beyond my sight, and I rarely know where we are going. But the ground is still beneath me, and the wolves are kept at bay, so He remains.

There was a time I thought the Valley was a place I could stumble into, or get lost, and end up in. But the Valley is simply where I'm going. Maybe I've always been there, and the shadows simply shift with the light and darkness. At times, the green pastures around me are plainer. At times, the waters are more still. But as long as I am in the Valley, there will be a shadow. And as long as it is only a shadow, the darkness of the Valley is not complete.

Beth Thielman

BALM

CUP OF TREMBLING

Both priest and prophet recognize
Redemption's light on holy eyes
Small cup of grief in Mary's womb,
Sword-piercing curse, portent of doom
With songs of praise they lift Him up
Who can drink all earth's trembling cup.

His final night He gave a sign:
And will you drink this cup of mine?
Betrayal comes before the day
As friends and fellows flee away
By one of you with whom I sup,
Now dipping in this trembling cup.

Life-giving spit drooling to mud
Smelling of tears, tasting of blood
Now in the flesh heaven will shine,
Drinking the dregs of hatred's wine.
Our fragile sorrows taken up,
Poured into night time's trembling cup.

Small cup of grief within each womb
For children born into a tomb,
Deep cup of trembling to the dead,
To those who feast on sorrow's bread
Heaven has drunk earth's trembling cup:
Now all our grief is swallowed up.

On the time-ending tree he's put
Unto hell's depths His cross takes root.
Gone, ancient chasm, shaken down
By the new seed His drinking's sown
To burning love of God brought up
For Heaven drank earth's trembling cup.

Summer Kinard

GOD, THE LORD IS MY STRENGTH; HE MAKES MY FEET LIKE THE HIND'S FEET, HE MAKES ME TREAD UPON MY HIGH PLACES.

HABAKKUK 3:19

STEADY

Who am I, now that the storm has passed? A measure of justice was granted to me by the Lord. Subjected to federal scrutiny, one of my abusers is now serving a sixty-year prison sentence because of what was uncovered with my uncertain cooperation. I was so afraid of how much I loved him. It nearly destroyed me to turn him over. I never thought that there would be a life beyond him.

Living in the aftermath is more challenging than living through the epicenter of my pain. I am always resting on the event horizon of grief, forever balancing between life and destruction. I get up, I say my prayers, and then I stumble from task to task. Before, my journey was a matter of survival. Now that my journey is a matter of living, I'm lost and ill equipped. How am I supposed to keep moving now that I don't know where I'm going?

Free will is more frightening than it ever has been. Everything was easier when I believed that God was a skilled puppeteer, ordaining all my choices. Fear freezes me to the spot, like a rabbit crouched in the underbrush. Life altering decisions swirl around me in a kaleidoscope of possibilities. This new kind of love is terrifying; I am possessed by anxiety. What if all my choices are the wrong ones?

I bless my body with the sign of the cross and dare to hope that my words may pierce the Theotokos' heart. Make my path like the doe's. Steady me through this rocky ravine, and though I am high and the way is treacherous, let me pass unharmed. I am called to love the Lord, even in my insufficiency and fear, and trust that He will make my feet like the hind's.

Stasia Braswell

TRULY, I SAY TO YOU, THERE ARE SOME STANDING HERE WHO WILL NOT TASTE DEATH BEFORE THEY SEE THE SON OF MAN COMING IN HIS KINGDOM.

MATTHEW 16:28

TRUST

As a child, I was told that Jesus is referring here to John, and the visions of Christ's return John would see in Revelation. Both then and now I consider this justification a travesty. I've heard alternate explanations since then – Jesus was talking about the Transfiguration, or Pentecost, or the destruction of Jerusalem. It doesn't matter; the point, in my mind, has always been that whether or not Jesus could claim his statement to be technically true, he knew he was making his disciples believe something that wasn't true at all.

God seems to do this all the time, and I've never been able to forgive him for it. He's always coming "soon," and 2,000 years later, we're still waiting. I have some experience with people who say they'll be back soon and then don't come back ever. My dad, for instance, left me somewhere around the beginning of my memories. You know how long it takes a two-year-old to figure out that "not now" actually means "never?" A really, really long time. There is nothing worse than a purposeful raising of false hope, except maybe how the fact that the false hope can be construed as true (if you squint) means that all the things it makes you feel are actually your fault for misunderstanding.

I was thirty-three before I realized that John 21:23 – which talks about how the rumor that John would live until Christ returned got started (and how it was a misunderstanding) – was written by...John. So, I guess maybe John didn't spend the rest of his life in blissful anticipation of Christ's return and then get a nasty shock when he died without it happening, only to have Jesus explain, "Oh, no, you totally misunderstood. That wasn't what I meant," which is what I had always imagined.

In that realization I am provided an opportunity: I can contemplate the possibility that God might be very different from the people in my life. And if John didn't mind what Jesus said, maybe I don't have to, either.

Catherine Hervey

THEN THE MOTHER OF THE SONS OF ZEBEDEE CAME UP TO HIM, WITH HER SONS, AND KNEELING BEFORE HIM SHE ASKED HIM FOR SOMETHING.

MATTHEW 20:20

CRINGE

I used to read this story and cringe. Any parent who attempts to live vicariously through his or her children risks becoming ridiculous. (The 2019 scandals involving celebrity parents trying to bribe their child's way into college come to mind.) The brazen way this mother advocates for her sons' worldly advancement is no different. Her audacious request – that Jesus grant brothers James and John the two places of highest honor in his kingdom – is so embarrassing. Clearly she has totally misunderstood the paradoxical nature of the Kingdom of God, where the price of admission is to become "like children" (Matthew 18:3) and where "many that are first will be last, and the last first" (Matthew 19:30).

Reading this story still makes me recoil, but this time the shame is my own. Though I'm not a parent, I can see myself in the wife of Zebedee, because I can't even count the number of times that I have done Jesus homage only because I wanted something. I approach prayer not in the freedom of pure intentions, simply to express my love for the Lord, but rather under duress, in poverty or in pain. Like the ambitious mother, I think I can gloss over my selfishness by putting on a show of piety. The worst part is that her intentions were almost certainly nobler than mine – she genuinely wanted what was best for her children and thought this was the best way to ensure their future happiness. I, on the other hand, seek my own success. I may be kneeling in a posture of humility, but I am asking for what I want instead of placing myself trustingly into God's hands.

Emily Byers

HOW LONG, O LORD? WILT THOU FORGET ME

FOREVER?

HOW LONG WILT THOU HIDE THY FACE

FROM ME?

PSALM 13:1

HIDDEN FACE

One night, when I encouraged my daughter to pray, I was not surprised to see her look down at her hands and mumble, "it never works." She struggles with anxiety. We've had this conversation before. I reminded her that prayer is not magic, it isn't asking and getting. Prayer is talking to God, spending time with him. The goal is to know God.

"But how can I get to know him if he never answers?" she asked. I reminded her of all the things in the world that fill her with joy and curiosity: lizards who lose their tails, meteor showers, the way dough turns into bread when it's baked. God designed and gave us all these things. She smiled briefly, but I knew that wasn't enough. She wants to know God is present in her life. She wants to see the evidence like the crust that forms on the bread in the oven. She wants to catch him like the lizard tail in her hand.

I've had those same thoughts. I was barely an adult when I saw my faith in its historical context for the first time. What I thought was absolute truth turned out to be 19th Century systematic theology. I had the choice to cede my curiosity or grasp steadfastly - even if it meant a painful break with what I'd always known.

I didn't know where my questions would lead, if I would find truth or silence. But I asked. I found doubt for many years. And eventually I found prayer. And incense. Chrismation. Community. Reconciliation. Joy.

I tell my daughter, sometimes knowing God begins with praying honestly, "How long will you hide your face from me?" And continuing steadfastly until eventually we can rejoice and sing, "he has dealt bountifully with me."

Laura Wilson

HE HAS STRENGTHENED THE BARS OF YOUR GATES; HE HAS BLESSED THE CHILDREN WITHIN YOU.

PSALM 147:13

THE SHADOW OF DEATH

It's getting easier to hear Psalm 147 these days. There was a time I felt it was mocking me: the time after our fifth child was born, after the hysterectomy and the days in the ICU, after the long, slow recovery and the two months of trips to the NICU to visit our tiny baby. I was 34. During those days, I would think of all the eggs still in my body, released on time each month but with no place to go. How could those "children within me" be blessed?

And then would come the guilt: we have five children. All of them, even the one born at 28 weeks, are healthy and smart and strong. What on earth have I got to complain about? Technically I am "infertile"; to say that with my flock around me seems like a bad joke.

Still. Every time one of my friends announces she's pregnant, there's a pang. I smile, and congratulate her, and ask how the morning sickness is going. I go through the motions. And I go home and cry, and pray for a more grateful heart. I remind myself that while abundance may soften suffering, it doesn't make it go away; it's not wrong for me to mourn my brokenness.

How has God blessed the children still within me? That's hard for me to see. It's true that the chances of more than one or two of them being born in any case were tiny, but somehow that's not very comforting.

The children within my gate, however, God has blessed abundantly: with loving hearts and beautiful talents, joyful laughs and comforting hugs. And I am grateful that, in many ways – hugs, LEGO creations, and ways I could not have imagined before I was a mother – God works among me and my children to slowly heal some of my brokenheartedness.

Christina Baker

FOR THE SAKE OF CHRIST, THEN, I AM CONTENT WITH WEAKNESSES, INSULTS, HARDSHIPS, PERSECUTIONS, AND CALAMITIES; FOR WHEN I AM WEAK, THEN I AM STRONG.

II CORINTHIANS 12:10

PERFECT IN WEAKNESS

I have been a woman who never allowed herself to portray weakness. From a young age, I taught myself to present my best foot forward and be wrapped in pride. I couldn't ask for help from anyone because I would always figure out and navigate everything. Asking for help was, for me, a sign of weakness. I was what you would call a self-made woman.

I remember inviting friends out to buy them dinner or have a fun time with the last of my money. If anyone needed anything from me—money, selling me things I didn't need, etc.—I would give or buy so that they didn't think I couldn't afford it.

Recently, when everything around me collapsed—lost my job and my relationship—didn't tell anyone. All this pretense put a weight on me, and all of sudden I succumbed to the spirit of heaviness. I was staying in bed for days, not showering, not eating, just crying and sleeping.

When I read this verse, it felt like I was seeing it for the first time. It freed me, and I held on to it! Being vulnerable and open was difficult. I'm still journeying. But I can now let people know when I'm facing tough moments. More than that, I can confidently surrender my weakness to God.

In acknowledging my weakness to Christ, I've seen his miracles and strength poured out so richly in my life. He has shown me that in my weakness, He's glorified when He lifts up my head. God doesn't expect me to have it all together, because his power is made perfect in my weakness.

Edith Adhiambo

THE LIGHT SHINES IN THE DARKNESS, AND THE DARKNESS HAS NOT OVERCOME IT.

JOHN 1:5

LIGHT IN DARKNESS

My vigil lamp hangs in the corner of our living room, so everyone knows when I've stood to light my lamp and pray each morning. But some mornings, like today, they know that I've avoided eye contact with the dark corner from which only the golden outline of Christ shines. The gold leaf reflects the morning sunlight from nearby windows; but his face is dark, the paint awaiting a flame to reveal his presence in the dark room.

I painted this icon of Christ. I applied that gold with tightly held breath and smooth fingers that masked my anxiety. I learned to write icons from faithful women, painters like me. I studied at a monastery, diligently taking notes, and came home to continue to practice this liturgical art. I am not a perfectionist, painting with such care is a struggle. Yet, I painted the wings of the archangels; I gessoed and sanded, gessoed and sanded smooth, curved boards for the Annunciation to Mary; I studied the patterns of highlights on the garments of the four gospel writers. I carefully learned the face of Christ himself. I was faithful to inscribe his image with precision in burnt sienna, napthol red, and 22 karat gold.

But I am not faithful enough to strike a match this morning.

Even though I can't see his face from the dark corner, I know his eyes are drawn with pupils centered in the iris so he is looking at me wherever I stand. I know his hand is raised in blessing whenever I'm ready to look upon him. The gift of icons – of Christ's very incarnation – taught me this. The image of the invisible God made visible. The God who is always present revealing himself. Despite my faithlessness, Christ's faithfulness calls me out of my darkness.

Laura Wilson

HELP

TAMAR TWICE-WIDOWED, ACCUSED

I.
date-sugar sweet   to sing
the righteous shall flourish
like the palm tree

        root-feet drink
                clear running freshet
        tree-head high
                to fire of sky

          fire to purple
        sugar-cluster fruit

(did Judah consider
        her sturdiness?)

II.
gleefully easy
        to blame the young bride
for death-work
        of the Lord:

death to Judah's firstborn,
death
  to second

death to each
        subtle thief

      who sees free sweetness
                        to take, to take
            sugar without weight

deliciously easy
        to turn aside, blind,
fabulate indefinite delay:
            tomorrow,   tomorrow,

wife non-wife wait
        bide time as a widow

III.
eyes gaze from the clusters of dates
        yes even trees

even skins of darkened tent
        at night had eyes to see

widow-wife waits where eyes will see
        wakens world to witness

eyes of the Lord
        every place

IV.
gleefully easy
        to wait
            at the crossroads
        to hide
behind public eye

(where eyes will see
what they want to see)

how sweet
        to take
security: signet,
   cord, staff;

how sweet in secret
ripening to wait

V.
Judah, mind the stone
in the fruit, mind arrival
        of tales, of eyes,
            of secrets to light,
mind your own marks
        of authority, fact:
signet, cord, staff;

DARKNESS IS AS LIGHT

Judah, judge rightly: irrigate
    pollinate   let every palm flourish
        for righteousness' sake
before the fire, before
the eyes of all, speak:
count your own unblinding
        as open-eyed reckoning
   justice as sugar-sweet

weigh your own professed
righteousness against hers:
eyes,   root,   fruit.

Allison Boyd Justus

THE SICK MAN ANSWERED HIM, "SIR, I HAVE NO MAN TO PUT ME INTO THE POOL WHEN THE WATER IS TROUBLED, AND WHILE I AM GOING ANOTHER STEPS DOWN BEFORE ME."

JOHN 5:7

DISABILITY LIFE

My disability life is a life shrouded with contradiction. I am living, yet dead. I am living to the fullness of my potential but stunted. I am as well as I can be, but seriously ill. If the Christian faith is about seeking stability, I fall short every day: I have rapid cycling bipolar II, which might as well be the antithesis of the peace of God. It is hard to fathom that I am made in the image of God when I am crafted with such a serious defect. It is hard to imagine that I am sustained by the Holy Spirit, flooded with the light of Christ, and a true Christian woman – unless, of course, I'm manic.

Christ took pity on the sick man, languishing beside the pool. The sick man seems to say, "Lord, I am trying to take care of myself, to bring healing to my soul and body, but I can't do it alone." This sentiment resonates within my bones. I am trying, Lord, but I am shackled. I am trying, yet my illness dominates my will. I can't fight my way free of it.

I am ashamed of my condition; mental illness makes one a pariah. Schizophrenia, personality disorders, and bipolar disorder are all frightening, strange, and alien to the average existence. Most people can say that they have experienced some form of depression or anxiety, but to be bipolar is to be beyond the pale.

I think of the man beside the pool, crying out to Christ, begging the Lord to bridge the spiritual gap between disability and wholeness. The only thing I know to do is to force myself to cling to my daily prayers to try and compel myself to stability. It is a herculean effort, like clinging to the cross in a hurricane.

Stasia Braswell

AND BEHOLD, A LEPER CAME TO HIM AND KNELT BEFORE HIM, SAYING, "LORD, IF YOU WILL, YOU CAN MAKE ME CLEAN."

MATTHEW 8:2

LIKE THE LEPER

In moments of discouragement, when I'm sinking fast beneath waves of grief or shame, I allow the enemy to trick me into believing that it's my responsibility to heal and strengthen myself. I forget that my sanctification is God's project, not mine, and I attempt to be self-sufficient instead of begging to be healed. I keep everyone at arm's length instead of taking refuge in community. One winter day several years ago, I'd sunk into a deep melancholy, and I was sick with a cold. I hadn't been able to pray in days. I had closed all of the curtains and blinds and was sitting alone in the dark when a friend came to check on me. The urge to shut him out was so intense that I almost refused to open the door. "Go away – " I started to say. "Please let me in," he said. When I opened the door a crack and saw his expression of tender concern, I realized: This is how the Lord comes to me, and this is how I push him away.

As a recovering perfectionist and overachiever, I may be more prone than most to stubborn self-sufficiency. The sense of satisfaction that comes from productivity is seductive, and it's easier to chase that feeling than it is to seek the Father's will. I don't ask to be healed, because I've grown accustomed to stumbling through life with my wounds. Asking for healing would force me to look at the sores covering my skin, and I'd rather not.

The leper approaches Jesus boldly and asks for a life-changing gift, and Jesus bestows that gift of healing willingly. Not only does He restore the diseased man's body, but He heals his broken heart as well by making it possible for the man to be reintegrated into society. God desires my healing; Jesus' prompt response to the leper's plea makes this clear. But He can only heal me when I approach Him in a posture of dependence, recognizing that I cannot cure my own disease. If, like the leper, I let the Lord touch my wound, I can open the door to others. I can let myself be loved, sores and all.

Emily Byers

AND BEHOLD, THE LORD PASSED BY, AND A GREAT AND STRONG WIND RENT THE MOUNTAINS, AND BROKE IN PIECES THE ROCKS BEFORE THE LORD, BUT THE LORD WAS NOT IN THE WIND; AND AFTER THE WIND AN EARTHQUAKE, BUT THE LORD WAS NOT IN THE EARTHQUAKE; AND AFTER THE EARTHQUAKE A FIRE, BUT THE LORD WAS NOT IN THE FIRE; AND AFTER THE FIRE A STILL SMALL VOICE.

I KINGS 19:11-12

IN THE QUIET

The Prophet Elijah's life is full of rain and fire, battles and miracles, but my favorite story is his encounter with God on Mt. Horeb. I've never slaughtered pagans or been forced to run for my life - but I have zealously spoken up when friends justified racism or misogyny, only to be labeled as partisan and faithless.

I'm no Prophet Elijah, but I relate to the heartbreak of his zeal, his exhaustion and loneliness in the face of the violence of his life, when he cried out to God: "It is enough now." "I am the only one left." It's a familiar mood.

But God visited Elijah in his heartbreak. He watched at the mouth of the cave as a violent wind rent the mountain, then an earthquake, then fire. God sent those, had power over them – but the Lord himself was in the gentle breeze that followed. This phrase is also translated "a still small voice," "a low whisper," even "the sound of silence." Not Paul Simon's silence, but one that was richly communicative. Whatever Elijah heard, it was quiet and gentle, and he knew the Lord was in it. This is what drew Elijah out, face covered in humility.

I'm moved by God's care for Elijah, making himself known in gentleness. God has power over the raging violence in my life, too. He's more powerful than the partisan division, the racial hatred, and the clever clap backs that break my heart. But God doesn't come to me in those; he comes in the quiet. When I watch for him, he draws me out of the flashy news cycle and the angry social media comments. Tenderly drawing me away from violence to gentleness, humbling me with my own silence, he makes his presence known.

Laura Wilson

AND A LEPER CAME TO HIM BESEECHING HIM, AND KNEELING SAID TO HIM, 'IF YOU WILL, YOU CAN MAKE ME CLEAN.' MOVED WITH PITY, HE STRETCHED OUT HIS HAND AND TOUCHED HIM, AND SAID TO HIM, 'I WILL; BE CLEAN.'

MARK 1:40-41

IF ANYONE; IF YOU

My gentle father just snapped one day. It took an ambulance and police officer just to get him to the hospital. He was screaming obscenities, his sentences were broken and garbled, and he was convinced everyone was out to get him. For weeks I deposited all my belongings into a locker before being escorted by security to visit my father in that part of the hospital no one sees: the locked mental ward.

It was such a cold place. No decorations. One tv. A few chairs and tables. Security officers watching every move. Moans, curses, crazy laughs filled the air as we followed my vacant father down one hall and back again while he angrily muttered disconnected sentences that had no bearing on reality. It was heartbreaking and terrifying.

On one such visit, as I waited for my father, a relative of mine remarked with disgust, "How could they keep him here with these people?" I was shocked. I know it was hard to grapple with the sickness my dad was experiencing, but wasn't he exactly like these people?

Leprosy may no longer exist in the First World, but there is a new, untouchable disease running through our streets: a broken mind. It fills people with horror, and they shy away as if mental illness were contagious. My father refused to let us tell his church about his illness, not even for prayer, so much of the burden fell on us to secretly care for him. The fear is: if anyone knew, they'd shun us. But oh, how we needed the touch of Jesus! Would a priest have come to see my dad in the locked ward? What would that have done for my dad, for me? One day, I hope that becomes the norm and not the exception.

A.N. Tallent

EVEN THE SPARROW FINDS A HOME, AND THE SWALLOW A NEST FOR HERSELF, WHERE SHE MAY LAY HER YOUNG, AT THY ALTARS, O LORD OF HOSTS, MY KING AND MY GOD.

PSALM 84:3

FAITHFUL

I walked over the frost-brittled grass, my long skirt swishing it dryly. I'd come to weep below the willows, to let the sound of the stream carry my lament with me. We'd just come home from our church, a community that had sent us overseas as missionaries for six years.

We didn't know we'd be coming home to a church that had unmoored itself from truth. We tried to sound the alarm, to throw an anchor over the edge, to stop the drift that was getting progressively worse. Running around on the deck, talking, pleading, praying; it didn't move the crew, though the fellow passengers were quietly, too quietly, in agreement. "Oh yes, we agree with you, but you know…"

We left our church. It felt like a divorce, a death. Visiting other churches throughout the next year was a Purgatory of Small Talk. I nearly printed a t-shirt that said, "Relax, I Love Jesus", because I just wanted to be invisible, not hyper-welcomed.

One of the churches we visited was unlike any other. There were candles, icons shining with gold leaf, ancient chants, and everywhere, beauty. This turned my husband into a cactus; prickly with irritation at all the high church strangeness. I knew down to my marrow that we were home.

Many nights I had stood alone in my prayer corner, tears streaming, longing to be knitted once again into a community of believers; one that I'd never have to leave as it had remained faithful for millennia. Five years passed of learning, praying, and fighting, five years for my children to find their way forward. I wept when they went under the baptismal waters, I wept as they received Holy Communion. God, in His kindness, turned my bitter tears into tears of radiant joy. He led us home.

Sarah Lenora Gingrich

HE WHO CLOSES HIS EAR TO THE CRY OF THE POOR WILL HIMSELF CRY OUT AND NOT BE HEARD.

PROVERBS 21:13

SOUNDING

Night had fallen and we were walking the dog when we noticed her sobbing, visibly needing help. She sat sprawled in the grass, rubbing her aching, swollen feet while the tears rolled down her cheeks. She asked, "What did I do to deserve all this pain?"

A child, close in age to our daughter, sat alone on our corner, afraid to go back to the group home she had run away from. "Why do I always make such bad choices?" she rhetorically scolded. She said her auntie died of sickle cell and her mom 'got depressed' and put her in the system. She lamented that no one would ever adopt her because she was high risk. When the police asked her age, she disclosed that she was twelve years old.

Abandoned by her friends, she was lost, exhausted, and afraid. She begged us to call the police and spoke plainly of suicide, maintaining that her life was pointless and that she mattered to no one.

As we waited, I felt the emptiness of what we could offer. Praying with her, I wondered that God had placed her by our home. I imagined Him, guiding her, bending His ear to her cry for help. She seemed hopeful, expectant that maybe our prayers would move God to help.

When the police arrived, she explained how scared she was but that somehow, she found us. She glanced at us. Was it recognition registering in her eyes that maybe God had *already* seen her? That He was there, present in us, sitting by her side? At that same moment I held her gaze, I saw Christ before me through her tears.

Later that night I pleaded with God, "Her cry is sounding in my ear but what am I supposed to do? Please send help."

Andrea Bailey

BEHOLD, AS YOUR LIFE WAS PRECIOUS THIS DAY IN MY SIGHT, SO MAY MY LIFE BE PRECIOUS IN THE SIGHT OF THE LORD, AND MAY HE DELIVER ME OUT OF ALL TRIBULATION.

I SAMUEL 26:24

STEALING THE SPEAR

The air stank from an unsteady wind that blew from the chemical plants and the paper mill in turn. My dad had been drinking as usual, but his ire was up because of the approaching holidays. Every year his ghosts became more real to him in late autumn. He tried to silence them by drinking. He tried to fight them by fighting us.

That night he was furious. His movements jerked with impatience and the taut wariness of adrenaline. He was raring for a fight. He pulled his pistol out and loaded it, glaring at me and my mother. The children were hungry because he had drunk away his paycheck, but he blamed us for the lack of food that proved his lack of responsibility. Before he could act on his rage, my grandmother pulled up in the driveway. She had brought money for food. He went outside to get the money and talk with her. He growled at me before he left, "That gun better be there when I get back." I glared and nodded.

As soon as he slammed the door behind him, I rushed to the pistol and opened it. I pulled out all of the bullets and put the gun back on the shelf, pointing at me as before. I put the bullets in the mostly-empty cupboard, behind two black and white canisters of government peanut butter. Dad used half of the grocery money to drink himself to sleep. I put the gun away but left the ammo hidden.

I don't have to let myself be fodder to other people's irrational rage, but neither should I strike against them. When internet harassers rise against me, I can choose to block them rather than firing back. When angry people accuse me falsely, I can stand firm without striking them. David stole Saul's spear. I stole Dad's bullets.

Summer Kinard

TRIAL

SHIFT:PLUNGE (AFTER PSALM 42)

Deep calls to deep at the roar of your waterfalls;
All your breakers and your waves have gone over me.
"Deep calls to deep" supersedes suicidal ideation.
Deep calls to deep, and deep answers: roar,
tumult, baptismal purge – dumb urge toward suffocation
dies; living submission arises as breath. No longer gunshot
but ocean's roll and roar, no longer freefall but rip current
into mightiest love, no longer rip but pierce and stitch;
self-impalement hesitates; pointed patient search
ensues; no longer drowning, but – no longer mere
drowning! Deep calls to deep, and foam and force
of torrent, joyful, severe, soda, steel wool,
rush alive to scour the base and inside of the skull,
unravel heart tissue, untangle veins, arrange anew and raw,
revive. It's a descent into death, all right – twisted wish
overpowered, drowned, scoured, rerouted, risen, rinsed.

Allison Boyd Justus

But Martha was distracted with much serving; and she went to Him and said, "Lord, do you not care that my sister has left me to serve alone? Tell her then to help me."

Luke 10:40

DOES HE CARE?

How unfortunate for Martha that her first recorded words in Scripture are a complaint! "Lord, do you not care?" She is only quoted in one other story: the raising of her brother Lazarus. Ever the know-it-all, Martha tells Jesus he's arrived too late and even interjects to remind him about the stench from the tomb before the stone is dislodged. It's almost as if all of her speech demonstrates the same disgruntled inner monologue: "Doesn't Jesus know? Doesn't he care?"

I've always had the impression that Martha wasn't a very pleasant person: always presuming she knows better than everyone else, always taking care of everything herself, always telling others what she decides they need to know. Basically, Martha is a control freak, and control freaks are difficult to love. Yet Scripture tells us Jesus "loved" Martha (John 11:5), just as he loved her siblings. She was his dear friend.

Perhaps calling Martha a control freak is unfair, but it takes one to know one. I'm an oldest child who's always been a know-it-all. In grade school, I was eager to answer any question the teacher asked because I presumed I knew the correct response. At church, I had a seat on every committee and ministry team, confident I could keep all the plates spinning. In my daily life, I'm constantly fighting the temptation to step in and "take care of" other people's problems, without stopping to consider whether or not I should. And this same pride permeates my spiritual life.

It's so easy to jump to the conclusion that I have a better perspective than Jesus, to cry out in frustration: "Doesn't he know? Doesn't he care?" – instead of believing that he loves me, even when I'm being an insufferable know-it-all.

Emily Byers

GOD IS LOVE.

1 JOHN 4:8

HE KNOWS OUR FRAME; HE REMEMBERS

THAT WE ARE DUST.

PSALM 103:14

KNOWING LOVE

What is love? Yes, I know, there's a long list in 1 Corinthians that says things like, "Love is kind, love is patient," etc., but what do those words really mean? From the very beginning of my life, love was fickle, unpredictable, and rare. There wasn't enough of it to go around. If you were to ask me about wrath or judgment, I could talk all day about the intricacies of appeasing an angry parent or feeling guilty about breathing. But love? What is love?

People tell me God's love is unconditional. Wow. What even is that? I live in a world where love is dished out in a reward system. Teachers loved me because I did what they said and worked hard. You get a raise for the same reasons. A girl might earn love by dressing modestly or immodestly, depending on the person involved. You receive love by agreeing with those in power and bending over backwards so they can get their way. You keep your head down and don't make waves, and maybe love will fall from their tables like miniscule crumbs for you to lap up greedily. Love always has strings attached.

I know, intellectually, that God loves me, that His love is unearned and limitless. But the words just bounce off my heart. They apply to other people, certainly, but me? I'm a mess! A spiritual misfit! Does He still love me if I don't meet His standards? My perspective of God has been damaged by the false portrayals of love that were fed to me as a child. I don't know what love really is, but I do know hope: Hope for a better future, hope for mercy and grace. I cling to hope that God sees what's been done to me and understands.

A.N. Tallent

I WILL RESTORE TO YOU THE YEARS WHICH THE SWARMING LOCUST HAS EATEN, THE HOPPER, THE DESTROYER, AND THE CUTTER, MY GREAT ARMY, WHICH I SENT AMONG YOU.

JOEL 2:25

GO BACK

When I walked out of my office that day, I intentionally turned off all feelings. It would be easier that way. But today, I laid face down on the carpet in front of my office door. I wanted to revisit that moment in time decades earlier when I chose emotional suicide.

I had to figure out how to survive. My physical, emotional, and spiritual strength was severely depleted. I needed physical strength to continue tending to my dying husband, and I desperately needed my intimate relationship with God which gave me the grace for what each day required of me. It seemed the best answer to lighten my load was to shut down emotionally.

I thank God that he didn't leave me in that place of emotional deadness. He invited me on a search and rescue mission to collect all the wounded parts of my being that were strewn along the path of my life. He took me on a journey back in time to locate unprocessed memories of anguish and loss that were like dangling threads causing me to stumble.

"Will you follow wherever I lead you? I am the One who guides you through this wilderness. I know you will fall, go in circles, and possibly quit, but as I look over my shoulder and see you, I will wait. If you are afraid you won't be able to keep up, I will circle behind you until your strength is renewed."

God assured me that once healed, those threads of traumatic memories would be woven into the beautifully unfolding tapestry of my life.

Sharon Ruff

DARKNESS IS AS LIGHT

FOR I KNOW THE PLANS I HAVE FOR YOU, SAYS THE LORD, PLANS FOR WELFARE AND NOT FOR EVIL, TO GIVE YOU A FUTURE AND A HOPE.

JEREMIAH 29:11

BREATHLESS

Our first fifteen years were filled with boats, kids, and everything outdoors. Our next fifteen years derailed when my husband was diagnosed with Chronic Progressive Multiple Sclerosis when he was thirty-five. Life as we had known it suddenly shifted. Our fast-moving train not only derailed, but the suspension bridge collapsed flinging us into unfathomable despair.

I was leaning against the wall in our hallway, a suitcase in each hand, after picking up our young sons from Grandma's house. She took care of them while we made the cross-country trip to Mayo Clinic and received the diagnosis. The boys were staring in shocked silence at their once robust father now crumpled in a chair.

Terror was etched on everyone's face during that frozen moment. I felt my only choice was to bury my own fear and attack this crisis with the ferocity of a first responder. I thought if my boys never saw me weak or crying it would help them not be afraid. I was wrong.

I desperately needed God's help to survive. Early in the morning I would slip into the extra bedroom, read and memorize scripture, and cling to words of hope to get through the day. But after years of my husband's continual decline, I reached the depths of despair.

"God I can't do this one more day," I cried. I had failed in my efforts to protect my sons. My own body was breaking down from caregiving. I urgently needed to hear from God. When I read that God had plans for me, I grabbed that sliver of hope and never let go.

Sharon Ruff

TAKE NO PART IN THE UNFRUITFUL WORKS OF DARKNESS, BUT INSTEAD EXPOSE THEM. FOR IT IS A SHAME EVEN TO SPEAK OF THE THINGS THAT THEY DO IN SECRET; BUT WHEN ANYTHING IS EXPOSED BY THE LIGHT IT BECOMES VISIBLE, FOR ANYTHING THAT BECOMES VISIBLE IS LIGHT.

EPHESIANS 5:11-13

THE LIGHT

There is a phenomenon in Japan known as hikikomori. It means "hidden forest," though, in this case, it refers to people, hundreds and thousands of people living in secret across the country. For whatever reason, they have become unable to face society and choose, instead, to hole themselves away in their homes, never to leave their rooms as a parent or loved one quietly leaves them food and pretends that they do not exist. The shame of their existence is too great, and so they disappear, often for years at a time.

I may never have locked myself away, but I know all about shame and the need to keep secrets. I loved when people came to visit our home, because then it meant my normally neglectful and abusive mother was suddenly fun to be around. Appearances, after all, had to be kept. The rule was: Don't talk about the abuse, the illness, or the pain. What's in the dark must stay in the dark...or else.

But this is not how things should be. Christ is Light; He exposes the darkness for all to see. When we keep quiet – whether about our abuse or grief or failings or sins or any negative experience – we lock it away like mold to fester and grow. Only by exposing it can we be healed, can we help others to heal. It takes courage to speak those words, make that appointment, open that door. There is true fear there. But it is the enemy of our souls who desires us to sit in our locked rooms of shame. Whatever darkness you are in, face it. Bring it to the Light. Fight for healing and for your own voice and never stop. You are not alone. He is here fighting for you.

A.N. Tallent

EVEN THOUGH I WALK THROUGH THE VALLEY OF THE SHADOW OF DEATH, I FEAR NO EVIL; FOR THOU ART WITH ME; THY ROD AND THY STAFF, THEY COMFORT ME.

PSALM 23:4

THE BURNING

I burned a house down while my eight-months pregnant friend was inside. I'd befriended Ruby on the streets while I was homeless for many months. She had managed to get into an apartment on the worst street in town. Ruby took me in, giving me the couch and a source of regular showers I needed in order to keep a meager job. We spent my first nights keeping dry in sharing our few dreams and hopes. Ruby made me godmother of the baby, as I was the one person she could count on.

I took the little money I had and spent it on food to make a homecooked meal – a real treat and a chance at normal after eating most of my meals from dumpsters on the street. That meal was my way to thank Ruby for giving me a chance to get back on my feet. While Ruby rested in the bedroom, I put the food in the oven and went to the store to get desert.

I heard the fire engines from inside the market several blocks away, but not until I got close to home, did I realize it was Ruby's house burning! I froze. Then I ran away. That night, I snuck down to a neighbor who told me that the food had caught fire, but she had gotten Ruby out in time. Ruby was treated for smoke inhalation, but the baby seemed to be okay. I never saw Ruby again. I was never godmother. That is what shame will do: Shame for nearly killing someone, for not being good enough, for falling below the standards of society and my parents, for not living my purpose. Shame for letting God down.

I wish I could say this was the end of a very dark tunnel, but it was the beginning, the initiation. At seventeen, I was just entering my valley of the shadow of death. Prayer kept me alive. Faith restored me. And fear, my constant companion for many years, lost its strength over me when I no longer believed in it.

Emry Sunderland

HE WAS DESPISED AND REJECTED BY MEN;

A MAN OF SORROWS, AND ACQUAINTED WITH GRIEF;

AND AS ONE FROM WHOM MEN HIDE THEIR FACES

HE WAS DESPISED, AND WE ESTEEMED HIM NOT.

ISAIAH 53:3

HE HID NOT HIS FACE

I was sitting at a red light, waiting to make a left turn. Next to the oncoming traffic a man was walking up and down with a sign. I couldn't read the sign, since his back was to me, but we all know what the sign said—something to the effect of "hungry" or "anything helps."

Then a police car stopped at the light. The blue lights flashed, and the officer flung his door open and stepped quickly out of the car. He called to the man with the sign, and waved him over. Between the two rows of cars, there was a conversation of which I could only see the outlines. The officer looked irate. When they were done talking, the man slunk over to a bench, sign gone or put away. The officer stormed back to his car, ripped the door open, and got back in.

Our light changed.

The whole scene might have taken a minute. Maybe there was some context there that I missed, though there was no law against panhandling in that area. One thing was clear, however: there was no kindness or concern for the plight of a fellow human being visible in the officer's body language. There wasn't even pity. There was contempt, self-righteousness, anger, disgust, and, as I realized laying awake in bed that night, violence. I did not feel safer for this officer's actions; I felt embarrassed. My initial thoughts were, "How could we?" and "God help us!"

Where is our compassion as a society, I wondered? Why do we insist on alienating and hurting our most vulnerable? Is this really how we treat Christ in the "distressing disguise of the poor"?

Christ was there, standing on the corner, despised.

I hid my face; I drove away.

Christina Baker

CONSOLATION

PLATYTERA (MORE SPACIOUS)

When we have waited
when we have withered
when the dust of our thoughts is strewn like breadcrumbs on barren hills
When hope's arrow has dulled
when sleep is not sleep
and waking is not waking
and seasons do not change
When the threads of the story are tattered
when dust veils what once shone
when voices echo
from corners of the endless night
we cannot see
When all our "whens" are stale
and the fields of faith are fallow
and the center is splintered
and we are all falling
and we are all reaching
and we are all clutching
When the shards of self are scattered
the bones of meaning dismembered
the ligaments of life distended
On that day let us be gathered
drawn together
as under wings or heavens or hands
more spacious than ours alone.
Let us return
to our selves
to one another
to the shores of a harbor we never left
or rather never left us.

Nicole M. Roccas

FOR MY FATHER AND MY MOTHER HAVE FORSAKEN ME, BUT THE LORD WILL TAKE ME UP.

PSALM 27:10

UNBROKEN

I was twenty-six when I found out my parents were filing for divorce. I was on my lunch break at work when Mom called to tell me. It wasn't shocking. She'd always talked of leaving my dad. They didn't get along, and now that my sisters and I were all out of the house, the timing was right. It all made perfect sense.

Ten minutes later, tears are streaming down my face. I have to go home. I can't think, can't even look into the mirror because in that face, in my very DNA, is the bond of two people, a bond that they have broken on paper, but which I cannot splice from my genes no matter how hard I try. I know it shouldn't matter. They're adults- I'm an adult - but the pain still comes out of nowhere, shattering everything about me.

I always knew my parents' marriage was a mess. Our family is a poster child of dysfunction, yet that foundation of a marriage, of knowing that at least my family was whole, had meant more to me than I realized. Now that was dead. How do you mourn a broken home? There's no coffin, no gravesite, no mourners to come alongside and help you along. Everything is the same outwardly, yet that relationship that caused my very existence has been destroyed. Where do I belong now? Who even am I?

When I first stepped into an Orthodox Church and saw the Virgin Mary and a plethora of other saints depicted on the walls, I suddenly realized I was home. Here was my family. Here was where I belonged. The natural family may be broken, but the spiritual family lives on, ever growing, inviting me in. And the gates of hell shall never break it.

A.N. Tallent

FEAR NOT, FOR I AM WITH YOU, BE NOT DISMAYED, FOR I AM YOUR GOD; I WILL STRENGTHEN YOU, I WILL HELP YOU, I WILL UPHOLD YOU WITH MY VICTORIOUS RIGHT HAND.

ISAIAH 41:10

EMBRACE

My words catch in my throat; it isn't easy to say such a thing; something that can sink one's standing, one's credibility. Nonetheless, I've come to expect and accept that God speaks how He wishes to with each of His children.

Visions are a messy business. Like warts perhaps. You don't really bring them up in conversation unless someone alludes to having them; you don't share your experience unless another does. Well then, keep your grain of salt at hand, dear reader.

The water was so dark, nearly black, and the waves rose and crashed over me. My limbs were leaden; they wouldn't move as I pleaded with them to. My face would pierce the skin of the brackish water just long enough to hear the roar of the storm, to suck in the smallest bit of air, before I was swallowed again by darkness. I will soon die, I thought.

A wave thrust my limp body high, and for one moment my head cleared the water, and I saw a man in a small wooden boat. He was coming for me. My face was pressed hard into coarse brown fabric, my breathing ragged and gasping, my hair dripping down the woolen fibers. I did not support my own weight; my limbs dangled, arms encircled my limp form against the steady rise and fall of the man's chest.

I didn't get to see the "how", the rescue, but I saw salvation; I saw my Rescuer. The vision ended, and I buried my face into my pillow, wishing myself back in His arms, safe. Again and again over the years my heart returns to that embrace, especially when I feel like the waves are stronger than my faith. Take heart, dear ones, He will help.

Sarah Lenora Gingrich

NOW I REJOICE IN MY SUFFERINGS FOR YOUR SAKE, AND IN MY FLESH I COMPLETE WHAT IS LACKING IN CHRIST'S AFFLICTIONS FOR THE SAKE OF HIS BODY, THAT IS, THE CHURCH.

COLOSSIANS 1:24

ASTONISHING

My kids love to hear the stories of the saints they were named after. St. Rose befriended the mosquitoes; St. Clare cut off her hair; St. Lucy's eyes were poked out, but they grew back! Saint stories include miracles, martyrdom, disobeying of parents...what's not to love?

When they ask me about my namesake, St. Christina, I hesitate.

St. Christina the Astonishing lived in twelfth century Belgium. She suffered seizures, and at the age of twenty-one she died, only to rise up and fly about the church during her funeral. She claimed that she had seen Hell, Purgatory, and Heaven, and that she could have stayed in Heaven, but chose to return to earth to suffer for souls. She spent the rest of her life begging, throwing herself into the freezing Meuse River, and escaping every attempt to confine her. She also went to great lengths to avoid other people—she said she couldn't stand the smell of their sins. She came to be regarded as a living saint, and died in a Dominican convent.

Though my modern mind struggles with parts of this story, there are days I empathize with St. Christina. Nap time failed. Everyone's bickering. Dinner is burning, because every three minutes I have to stop the baby from climbing something. The smell of sin is strong on all of us, and the temptation to abandon my domestic church and lock myself in my room gets stronger by the minute.

But St. Christina knew suffering was redemptive: her sacrifices could help souls in Purgatory ascend to Heaven. As Saint Paul reminds the church at Colossae, our sufferings are not useless. Joyfully borne, they help us to grow in faith, and contribute to the sanctification of Christ's mystical body, the church. With my patron saint in mind, I unlock my door and try to rejoice in my sufferings – one diaper, one toddler squabble, one sleepless night at a time.

Christina Baker

THE LORD IS NEAR TO THE BROKENHEARTED,

AND SAVES THE CRUSHED IN SPIRIT.

PSALM 34:18

TAKEN UP

There is an icon on the wall of our church of St. Mary of Egypt. Wan, worn, ribs jutting, white hair falling in clumps, threadbare robe askew, she reaches for the Eucharist held out to her by a priest. She had been a prostitute, wantonly throwing herself into that profession at the tender age of 12 until, many years later, she found herself at the door of a church begging the Mother of God to let her in and help her find forgiveness. Soon after, she left for the desert where she lived out the rest of her life fighting her inner demons and seeking the face of God, becoming an amazing woman of supernatural faith and ability.

We know now, in our modern era of psychology, that early promiscuity tends to spring from the scars of childhood trauma. Had St. Mary been sexually abused as a child? Did something heinous happen to make her run away from home to sell her body? We may never know. But, whatever the reason, she was terribly broken and hurting, and yet today her memory is so powerful that her story is celebrated every year during Lent. She was deeply scarred, and yet God did not shun her. He healed her.

When I was chrismated and about to receive my first Orthodox communion, I was absolutely terrified. But I looked at that icon, and I felt her presence. I, too, am broken. I, too, was abused and have a twisted concept of love. I struggle against so much, so many inner demons that scream out how worthless I am. But I felt her gentle presence guiding me toward the cup as a friend who understood that God does not reject the broken. He heals them and holds them close.

A.N. Tallent

BY DAY THE LORD COMMANDS HIS

STEADFAST LOVE;

AND AT NIGHT HIS SONG IS WITH ME,

A PRAYER TO THE GOD OF MY LIFE.

PSALM 42:8

SONG

I watched bluish flames burn like a pillar of eyes by my bedside when I woke in the middle of every night of my early childhood. He was my guardian angel, but I called him my Eyeball Man. When I was most in danger from my abusive family, I could see him there even before I fell asleep at night. It was his song, "Holy," that taught my heart the fear and love of God so that I learned to love Christ before I knew Him.

When my youngest son was born with a dangerous birth defect and had open abdomen surgery at two days old, I could do little for him. Time in the NCCU passed without day or night as I watched over him, praying and touching him as much as his support devices allowed. I couldn't feed my son while he recovered, but I could give him song as he slept through the night of healing.

Not knowing whether he would live or die, I sang him the most beautiful songs I knew – arias, hymns, tumbling motifs from oratorios, sturdy ancestral melodies that wore whichever words my weary heart could muster. I sang great arias about hope and love, my operatic soprano voice strained to the thinnest dolcissimo for my tiny boy, the fragility of melody mirroring the fragility of his life. In the space between my son and I, every song transformed into the blessing that angels never cease to sing. We sang, we heard, we were: holy.

Summer Kinard

THE STEADFAST LOVE OF THE LORD NEVER

CEASES,

HIS MERCIES NEVER COME TO AN END;

THEY ARE NEW EVERY MORNING;

GREAT IS THY FAITHFULNESS.

LAMENTATIONS 3:22-23

GREAT IS THY FAITHFULNESS?

Lamentations 3:22-23, and "Great Is Thy Faithfulness" – the verses and the hymn inspired by it, are everywhere in Christian life and kitsch. But those verses are sandwiched between some really hard verses and chapters – the kind you'd expect in a book titled "Lamentations," but not as wall art.

Five verses before: "My soul is bereft of peace, and I have forgotten what happiness is." The final verses of the book are, "Restore us to thyself, O Lord, that we may be restored. Renew our days as of old! Or hast thou utterly rejected us? Art thou exceedingly angry with us?"

The whole of Lamentations has a much different tone than its two most popular verses, and so may our lives. Five years ago, we moved to a new city for my husband to pastor at an urban church. We knew the position and location would be challenging, but I remember thinking, "We're sacrificing for Jesus, he'll reward us." Reader, our old house didn't sell. The senior pastor resigned. We had other staff issues. Friends left the church. The news cycles triggered serious depression for me as a sexual abuse survivor. We were living a much less gruesome version of Lamentations. Many days, I couldn't see any new mercies in the morning, and my soul had no peace or happiness. In the bleak times, I just hung on, doing what I had to do, hoping it was okay to be a pastor's wife just going through the motions.

A grueling five years later, I have learned that those motions – nightly prayers with my children and weekly worship with communion – sustain me until the days when glimmers of hope shine. As these cycles continue (some not as bad as others, now, thank you, Zoloft), I have come to realize that Jesus himself is my reward and my portion (as 3:24 says), no matter our material circumstances or my mental health. He has always been, and will always be, holding on to me.

Emily Hubbard

THEN HE SAID TO THE DISCIPLE, "BEHOLD, YOUR MOTHER!" AND FROM THAT HOUR THE DISCIPLE TOOK HER TO HIS OWN HOME.

JOHN 19:27

HEARTBEAT

One of the greatest delights and treasures of my conversion to Holy Orthodoxy was discovering the Mother of God. The Theotokos, she who is wider than the heavens, is not only Christ's mother but my mother. Christ gave her to us as an example of purest piety and for our protection and salvation. I struggle to feel close to either of my parents. I couldn't even process God as a loving father before I knew the Theotokos as a loving mother.

Yet, I forget that she is mine and that I am hers; grief and trauma have broken my grasp on other safe parents; sometimes, especially in the depths of my grief, I forget that she's even there. But I always find my way home. The Mother of God, the most treasured creature in existence, loves me more than I'll ever know in this lifetime. I pray that in Heaven, I'll be able to commune with her in fullness.

I imagine myself as a little girl, still learning about the ways of the world and my place within it, clutching my mother's hand. When I weep from grief, wail from frustration, scream in anger, I imagine that she scoops me up like a baby and enfolds me in her arms, wrapping her mantle securely around me. The saints entreat us to cling to her skirts. I imagine this too, dark fabric balled up in my fat baby fist, following my mother through daily life and past the greatest of threats.

Sometimes, when I can't settle myself down and I'm alone in my grief, I play the sound of a human heartbeat on YouTube. I remember that her breasts nursed the God of the universe and that she soothed His tears by holding Him to her chest. This mystical connection to Christ as both His child and His sibling in His inheritance as a child of God the Father is more profound than words can convey. She is His mother; she is my Mother. She is the safest of havens.

Stasia Braswell

CLOSER

BATH-JEPHTHAH'S WILDERNESS RITE

Two months two months   enough time for divine intervention   ram caught
in a thicket deliver our laughter bargain or no bargain

If I'd made the vow Jephthah would have cancelled it chided my misguided zeal
desperate over-devotion   foolish effervescence

The vow is a vow & I am a daughter of Sarah if I do not fear what is frightening
I am a daughter of Shiphrah and Puah if I resist by hiding the helpless

Am I a daughter of Sarah if I see a warrior as helpless   When I was a child
I admired those midwives of Egypt who sheltered delivered and lied

I love these mountains their wildness   their height
Two months a window, narrow threshold rises mountain-wide

When I was a child I say because that is not this let me meet my maker a woman
A vow is a vow I will not defy but among women alone I greet my nubility
Let it be said I first roamed the mountains with these I love as sisters
Give me two swelling moons I'll return fiery bride for true victor

I look up at the stars and know I am none of them   I birth no new light
Let me mutate, perfumed, become flame immolate immaculate

Enoch walked with God, and he was not   God took him
Take me

I do not yield my spirit without ceremony incendiary balm   or song
Let it be said I was with the wild beasts   and saw angels

Let it be said I wore balsam and white   and ascended
a ladder of fire

Allison Boyd Justus

DARKNESS IS AS LIGHT

FOR TO ME TO LIVE IS CHRIST, AND TO DIE IS GAIN.

PHILIPPIANS 1:21

ORDINARY MARTYRDOM

I had a dream. I walked into a room and Christ was there, tending icons as if they were pictures of old friends. I asked Him about the saints, who they are. He said that all of them were very different, and the only thing they had in common was a burning love for Him. At that point I woke up, and told Him that because of my autism, I can't feel this burning love people talk about, and I'm afraid I'm not cut out to be a saint like the martyrs in the icons.

He said to remember what St. Paul wrote: to live is Christ, and to die is gain. That's why, He said, the martyrs could be calm facing death, because they knew that through the torture and death lay Christ. I asked if it was the same as when I was depressed and suicidal and living for so long in that dark place. He was there with me, and yet when I finally came out of it, He went with me – I was simply going from one place to the other, in His company. He said yes, like that, but because of having been in that dark place, 'to live is Christ' is also a way of being a martyr.

From the lives of the saints, I had the impression that living with Christ is supposed to be *hard*. You have to fight and starve yourself to death and live in the desert for years and then maybe you get rewarded with this burning feeling of love and such...but I have no burning deep love – I don't even know how I'd recognize it. Being with Christ is so ordinary and comfortable. Even when I get hyper-focused on other things, He always eventually somehow drops by and gets my attention without being angry about it.

I hate touch. But sometimes I can feel Him hold my hand and it doesn't hurt.

Monica Spoor

DARKNESS IS AS LIGHT

THE PEOPLE WHO SAT IN DARKNESS HAVE SEEN A GREAT LIGHT, AND FOR THOSE WHO SAT IN THE REGION AND SHADOW OF DEATH LIGHT HAS DAWNED.

MATTHEW 4:16

GOSSAMER

Darkness really can walk right into your home, the door banging open, barely clinging to its hinges, walls reverberating. It can suck the air from the room, eviscerate at will, and steal what it wants. It comes as a crushing diagnosis, a betrayal, violence, an untimely death. In that moment there is a before and an after in one's life. The life of yesterday and the strange life of today. One feels hollowed-out.

Oh, God, says the soul, but I prayed...but I worshipped...why have You, who love me, permitted this destroying guest to assail me? Oh, God, why?

There is no way to move the darkness. Scream and tear at its black, papery robes, and you find your hands full of hot, black dust, and the darkness is unmoved, unscathed, maybe smirking. No pleading avails. No denial is strong enough to mask it.

I was curled up on the floor in my prayer corner, tears streaming one after another down my face. They came not from my eyes, it seemed, but my very marrow. I clutched a small icon of the Theotokos and Christ like a lifeline to keep me from drowning completely in my grief. I do not come to you with words that have not been burned into my heart. I say this from the valley.

No, the darkness cannot be moved, but...

...the light can be increased. We underestimate the power of our weak, feeble, barely-audible prayers, for we forget that one prayer holds hands with the one that follows, and as our fingers slip from one knot on our prayer rope to the next, so does God take hold of the strand of gossamer prayers, and comes near us, dispelling the darkness, little by little. Dear sisters, pray!

Sarah Lenora Gingrich

IF I SAY, 'LET ONLY DARKNESS COVER ME,

AND THE LIGHT ABOUT ME BE NIGHT,'

EVEN THE DARKNESS IS NOT DARK TO THEE,

THE NIGHT IS BRIGHT AS THE DAY;

FOR DARKNESS IS AS LIGHT WITH THEE.

PSALM 139:11-12

GOTH

I didn't wake up one morning and decide to be gothic. I doubt any goth ever has. I was told I was gothic by a girl in high school who was being lauded for how "diverse" her birthday sleepover was by a friend. "Even the goth girl is here!" To be fair, they didn't mean it in a derogatory way, but they clearly meant me. I was stunned. I remember going home and looking through all my clothes shocked to realize that, yes, I suppose most of them are black. When did that happen?

If there's one thing that unites gothic people, it's darkness, and I don't mean just the way we dress. The clothing is a consequence, a symbol of something greater. I've always told people that I'm in mourning; perpetual, deep mourning born from staring into the dark chasms of this world whether it be abuse, poverty, abandonment, betrayal, pain, etc. Gothic people understand the darkness. We didn't choose it. Oftentimes we were born into it, afflicted by the ones who were supposed to love us the most. We've been disillusioned with the idea that as long as you work hard and don't hurt anyone, life will be ok. That's simply not true. Satan rules this world- albeit his time is (thankfully) short. And somehow, someway, we have all stared into that darkness and been scarred.

Many people are afraid of goths. I've been called evil and witchy before, but I've never questioned the fact that God does not pull away from my clothing. He made the dark and called it good, and in my darkness is His light. Without that light, how could I ever survive what I've seen and experienced? Others may pull away, but thank God He never will.

A.N. Tallent

DARKNESS IS AS LIGHT

NOW AFTER THE SABBATH, TOWARD THE FIRST DAY OF THE WEEK, MARY MAGDALENE AND THE OTHER MARY WENT TO SEE THE SEPULCHER.

MATTHEW 28:1

BEFORE DAWN

Suffering is both an intimate and universal affair. My innocence was visited with violence. Someone took it upon themselves to perpetuate the familial curse of molestation on my tiny, preschooler body. God calls me by name and says that I am redeemed, but what use is that to me now, in the vast chasm of trauma? God allows great suffering for the sake of our salvation; it's mystical, mysterious, sickening. How could a Father allow such grief to exist if love is perfect? I am called to love Him, but I falter. All feels empty and fallen.

I've learned that God draws near during crisis. He is with us in the furnace. True suffering occurs in the aftermath, when all that is left are the ashes. But I take comfort in the women that have come before me; the holy myrrh-bearers did not know grief until their Lord was taken from them. Even so, they prepared to anoint His lifeless body. They held fast to their God even when He left them. They could not have known that He was harrowing Hell for their eternal salvation. With their earthly senses, they only knew that He was gone.

And yet, they chose Christ.

And yet, they chose hope.

Hope is not a subjective experience, but a crown of martyrdom, an orientation towards truth and beauty that chooses Christ and Christ again. Even when there is every indication that I have been abandoned, hope is an action, a ritual, a process. It is never a feeling, but a choice. Hope is a patient endurance of emotion, of grief and suffering and failure. Hope is repentance. Turning back, getting up, and choosing Christ. Even when I'm blind and stumbling, when God feels distant and silent: Christ is harrowing and hallowing the grave.

Stasia Braswell

THE SCRIPTURE SAYS, "NO ONE WHO BELIEVES IN HIM WILL BE PUT TO SHAME."

ROMANS 10:11

UNASHAMED

I have lived the past few months in fear of shame: of the shame that would come to me when the landlord came to kick me out because I have been struggling to pay rent; of the shame that would come to me when friends found out I lost my job months ago and have remained unemployed since then; of the shame of having to, for the first time in my life, continually ask for help from family and borrow from friends in order to get by; of the shame of my singleness glaring at me while friends marry, get married, have children, and establish their lives.

The last few months have been months of tears, fears, and despair. I believed that God was letting me go through all this to teach me a lesson, so I started not only having suicidal thoughts but reading articles that propagated suicide.

One afternoon, I decided to read the book or Romans. I came to Romans 10:11, then realized my fears had been from the Enemy. As long as I trust in God, I will never be put to shame. Shame will never come at my door. Jesus already died for my shame. He endured the cross, despising the shame so that I would never be ashamed in my life. My Father will not let me, his dearly loved child, know shame.

Shame has no place in my life, because I trust in God. It can be difficult; it will certainly be difficult; but I will not fear that any situation in my life will make me ashamed. Now I live in confidence knowing that no one who believes in him will be put to shame.

Edith Adhiambo

THEN PETER CAME UP AND SAID TO HIM, "LORD, HOW OFTEN SHALL MY BROTHER SIN AGAINST ME, AND I FORGIVE HIM? AS MANY AS SEVEN TIMES?" JESUS SAID TO HIM, "I DO NOT SAY TO YOU SEVEN TIMES, BUT SEVENTY TIMES SEVEN."

MARK 18: 21-22

YOU WANT ME TO WHAT?

Forgiveness: a word so easily thrown around in our Christian society. We're supposed to love our enemies and turn the other cheek. We all know this. I think it's easy to forgive the person who cuts you off in traffic, the rude client, the finicky boss, or the belligerent child. Sometimes, that's all people seem to consider when they hear Jesus' command to forgive. However, when I hear it, I get angry.

"Jesus," I want to say. "What about the abuser? The rapist? The pedophile? The betrayer? The absent parent? The tyrant? The murderer? What about the person who took my love and spat on it, not just once but day after day after day? What about the person who destroyed a loved one of mine, without remorse? What about the grief I can never let go of because of them? Or the mental, emotional, and even physical disabilities I'll carry for the rest of my life because of one person's ego? Jesus, this person ruined my life, and they're not even sorry! Jesus, I still have to face this person who refuses to acknowledge my pain, let alone their own sin! Jesus, you want me to forgive them?!"

I know His answer. I know He's forgiven all of that and worse in His infinite kindness and love. But I don't have infinite kindness and love. I have anger, hurt, trauma, post-traumatic stress, a deep scarring of the mind and spirit. How does one forgive those who inflict such deep wounds? How does one forgive oneself for trusting, making excuses for, or enabling such people? I don't have the answers to those questions, though I desperately wish I did. All I can do is wait for Him to show them to me as I cry, "Lord, have mercy!"

A.N. Tallent

AND HE DREAMED THAT THERE WAS A LADDER SET UP ON THE EARTH, AND THE TOP OF IT REACHED TO HEAVEN; AND BEHOLD, THE ANGELS OF GOD WERE ASCENDING AND DESCENDING ON IT!

GENESIS 28:12

THE WAY

My parents were fighting in the kitchen. Dad's deep shouts, Mom's wails, the crash of glass jars from the refrigerator, filled the air at every octave. Over that soundtrack of cacophony, I sang to my baby sister where I had hidden her in the back of my closet. If Dad came for us, I hoped he wouldn't see her. If he killed Mom, I would have to jump through the window with my sister. I would probably survive, and she would be safe.

That night, Dad left to get drunk after only a few punches. In the silence that followed, Mom took my baby sister to the living room. I closed the door behind her and stood in my room, my ears ringing. I told God I needed out.

Suddenly, I saw a ladder reaching up to heaven, by the door to the closet, in that violent house. The lower rungs were covered in razors and knives. It would be excruciating to climb, but I would reach God by it. Through the stench of fear and beer and nicotine, I caught a scent of heaven. I nodded my head to God and reached out to grab the lowest rung, felt the first cut focus my soul. The vision faded, but I kept climbing.

I went to college, the first in my family. I read the story of St. Perpetua, and I recognized her vision: the same ladder of blades, the way of pain. I had sheltered my sister, and St. Perpetua had sheltered me. I whispered, "Thank you," and sweet fragrance rose to meet me. With the sweetness, a truth: the ladder was Christ.

Summer Kinard

ABOUT THE AUTHORS

EDITH ADHIAMBO

Edith Adhiambo is a Christian Woman who lives in Nairobi, Kenya.

ANDREA BAILEY

Originally from Wisconsin, Andrea spent the past seventeen years in Lancaster, PA, before returning to her homeland of cheese and lakes. She is an Orthodox Christian, a wife, and a mother of six children. Andrea is a former director of an English language program for refugees and English language learners in her community, which she devoted her heart and soul to for eight years. She loves trees, lakes, animals, reading, writing, painting, gardening, and making soap. Andrea holds a Bachelor's degree from Briercrest College and an English as a Foreign Language certificate from Wisconsin English as a Second Language Institute. Presently, her primary work is facilitating healing at home. When circumstances allow, she attempts to write honestly about this life given to her, her faith, and the ways that her family's adoption journey has forever changed her understanding of love.

CHRISTINA BAKER

Christina Baker is a writer, mother, and homeschooler from Lafayette, Louisiana. She holds a B.A. in Latin and Classical Studies from Tulane University, and she studied Early Christianity for a year at the University of Notre Dame. She has a poem forthcoming in Highlights Hello magazine. Her essays appear in the Mighty Is Her Call blog. You can read more of her work at whiletheyweresleeping.com.

STASIA BRASWELL

Stasia Braswell is a student of psychology, philosophy, and theology. She bakes, she knits, she sings. Stasia is currently enrolled in an undergraduate college in the middle of nowhere, hoping that her degree will get her somewhere. She has been formally Orthodox for two years but called to Christ all her life.

EMILY BYERS

Emily Byers is a consecrated virgin in the Catholic Church, a vocation that revives a tradition from apostolic times when certain women experienced a divine invitation to sacrifice marriage and offer their virginity to God. On behalf of Jesus Christ and the entire Church, her bishop received her resolution to live a life of perpetual chastity in a public liturgy in 2012. Since her consecration, she has taught full-time at a local Catholic school, and she also assists young women who are discerning a possible religious vocation. She studied Spanish and Creative Writing at Louisiana State University and earned an M.A. in Theological Studies from Notre Dame Seminary in New Orleans. Find more of her writing at aconsecratedvirgin.wordpress.com.

BEV COOKE

Bev Cooke is an Orthodox Christian freelance writer and editor. She is author of akathists including the Akathist to St. Mary of Egypt; Akathist to the Theotokos, Healer of Hardened Hearts; and the Akathist to St. Emmelia for Our Lost Lambs (Coming 2021 with Park End Books). Her novels include *Feral* (Orca Book Publishers, 2008), *Royal Monastic* (Conciliar Press, 2008), and *Keeper of the Light* (Conciliar Press, 2006). Find more of Bev's writing at https://bevnalabbeyscriptorium.wordpress.com/. Bev and her husband live in British Columbia Canada in servitude to the Ruler of the Household, Sam the Cat.

SARAH LENORA GINGRICH

Sarah resides in Lancaster, Pennsylvania with her husband and large brood of children. She owns a soap company, gardens, and speaks shamelessly with her chickens, rabbits, and bees. Her first book, *Letters for Pilgrimage: Lenten Meditations for Teen Girls*, releases in 2021 with Park End Books.

CATHERINE HERVEY

Catherine holds an MFA in fiction from the Sewanee School of Letters and has written for Books and Culture and The Curator. She is currently a columnist for Ruminate and a 2020 Emerging Writer at the Collegeville Institute.

EMILY HUBBARD

Emily Hubbard is from Mississippi but now lives in St. Louis, where her husband pastors a multiethnic church. She loves sociology, public education, reading, crocheting, gardening, and sertraline.

ALLISON BOYD JUSTUS

Allison Boyd Justus, a poet from Tennessee, is the author of *Solstice to Solstice to Solstice: A Year of Sunrises in Poetry* (Alternating Current Press, 2017), currently pursuing a Master of Fine Arts degree in Creative Writing and Environment at Iowa State University. She holds a Master of Arts degree in New Testament Studies (Freed-Hardeman University, 2009), and her writing has appeared or is forthcoming in *High Shelf Poetry, The Showbear Family Circus, Shift: A Publication of MTSU Write, Lyrical Iowa, Penwood Review, Madcap Review, Quail Bell Magazine, Contemporary American Voices*, and elsewhere.

SUMMER KINARD

Summer Kinard is senior editor of Park End Books. She is an Orthodox Christian author and workshop leader specializing in accessibility and the theology of disability. In her blog posts and her latest book, *Of Such is the Kingdom: A Practical Theology of Disability* (Ancient Faith Publishing, 2019), Summer brings her extensive background in church history and theology (B.A. in religion, M.Div., Th.M. in early church history and theology) to skillfully weave together the healing patterns of Holy Tradition with the daily patterns of life with disabilities. Her other devotional work appears in *Seven Holy Women: Conversations with Saints and Friends* (Ancient Faith Publishing, 2020). Summer has an Adverse Childhood Experiences Score of 9/10. She is a cycle-breaker who bears witness to the goodness of the Lord, who works everything together for our salvation. She lives with her husband and their five children of joy in Texas. Read more of Summer's work at SummerKinard.com.

PHOEBE FARAG MIKHAIL

Phoebe is the author of *Putting Joy into Practice: Seven Ways to Lift Your Spirit from the Early Church* (Paraclete Press, 2019). She blogs at Being in Community (beingincommunity.com), and she teaches writing at Fairleigh Dickinson University. Phoebe is a clergy wife in the Coptic Orthodox Church and the mother of three children.

LYNNETTE AKINYI OCHIENG

Lynnette Ochieng is an IT Administrator by profession. She is a thirty-two-year-old, beautiful African lady who resides in the small city of Kisumu, in Kenya- East Africa. Lynnette graduated from Kampala University with a Bachelors in Computer Science and Information Technology. Lynnette enjoys reading during her free time, listening to music and dancing. She is part of the worship and intercessory team in her local church. She is fluent in Swahili and English languages, both written and spoken. She is currently learning French.

REE PASHLEY

Ree has many titles including; coffee-lover, Mama, and poet - but above all, she belongs to God.

NICOLE M. ROCCAS

In addition to working as the communications coordinator for The Canadian Council of Churches, Nicole M. Roccas, PhD, is a writer and podcaster intent on speaking meaning into deep suffering and grief. Her books include *Time and Despondency: Regaining the Present in Faith and Life* (Ancient Faith Publishing, 2017), *Under the Laurel Tree:*

Grieving Infertility with Saints Joachim and Anna (Ancient Faith Publishing, 2019), and *A Journal of Thanksgiving* (Ancient Faith Publishing, 2020). She also contributes to Ancient Faith Ministries as host of the Time Eternal podcast and blog and the Help My Unbelief podcast, which she produces with her husband. She has her PhD in European History from the University of Cincinnati and lives in the Toronto area, where she is active in several Orthodox communities. You can find more of her writing at nicoleroccas.com.

KRISTINA ROTH

Kristina Roth is a freelance editor and writer, an Orthodox Christian, and solo mom to an amazing boy. They live in the Black Hills of South Dakota. Please visit her at www.kristinatrue.com or on social media.

SHARON RUFF

Sharon Ruff lives in Michigan near her children and grandchildren. Her season of widowhood has been filled with grace after many years of caring for her husband who suffered from MS. She has served in women's ministries through Bible studies, retreats, personal ministry, as well as women's conferences in Ukraine and Africa.

MONICA SPOOR

Monica Spoor is an Orthodox Christian. She holds a Bachelor's of Theology from the Evangelische Theologische Hogeschool in Ede and resides in Veenendaal, the Netherlands.

EMRY SUNDERLAND

Emry Sunderland holds degrees in writing and history; she is a compassionate naturalist and advocate for self-responsibility in creating an abundant future. Her work has appeared in *APT* (Climate issue), *Qutub Minar Review*, and more. Read more from Emry at emrysunderland.yolasite.com.

A.N. TALLENT

A. N. Tallent is a gothic, stay-at-home mom and an Adult Survivor of Narcissistic Abuse and Child Abuse. Writing is her passion and an outlet that has seen her through many difficult years. Her life's dream is to marry her writing, experiences, and faith in a way that could help encourage and inspire others. She spent most of her childhood in Pennsylvania before moving to Florida at age twelve where she eventually married her high school sweetheart and graduated from a Christian, evangelical, Bible college with a B.A. in Missions. After several misadventures, cross-country moves, and daring escapes, she found herself converting to Eastern Orthodoxy and was chrismated at St. John Chrysostom Antiochian Church in 2018. She loves reading, tabletop RPGs, painting, video games, singing, birds, and tornadoes. She currently lives in York, Pennsylvania with her fabulous husband and adorable daughter, but she left a part of her heart in Japan.

BETH THIELMAN

Beth Thielman is a lifelong writer. Her body of work includes blogging, creative writing, and marketing content. She is an Orthodox Christian with an abiding interest in theology, literature, travel, and good conversation. Beth lives in her hometown of Nashville, Tennessee, with her husband, John.

LAURA WILSON

Laura Wilson is a painter and designer, homeschooling mother of three daughters, and a PhD student with an MTh in Applied Orthodox Theology. Her diverse background is the result of a daughter of a fundamentalist minister reclaiming joy from abstraction, and as a woman of faith, finding it in repentance and the complexity of spiritual and material existence.

ABOUT PARK END BOOKS

Park End Books is a traditional small press bringing to market accessible curricula and emerging Catholic, Orthodox, and other creedal Christian authors. Visit us online at ParkEndBooks.com.

COMING SOON FROM PARK END BOOKS:

Apocalypse: Managed by Jonathan Andrew (November 2020)

This humorous fantasy novel follows a close-knit group of friends and control freaks through the last day of Earth. Deeply insightful and laugh out loud funny, Jonathan Andrew's book is reminiscent of the styles of both C.S. Lewis and Douglas Adams.

Our Autistic Home by Summer Kinard (December 2020)

Learn how to make your household into a place where autistic family members thrive. Kinard brings the wisdom garnered from life in an all-autistic household to help families plan, adapt, understand, and remove handicaps to autistic functioning so that everyone feels truly at home. With the easy to apply tips and resources in this book, you can start a new era of joy for your entire family.

Letters for Pilgrimage: Lenten Meditations for Teen Girls by Sarah Lenora Gingrich (February 2021)

These seven weeks of letters engage the imagination and anchor the senses in stories that help awaken faith for teens on the Lenten journey. Evocative linocut illustrations by noted artist Ned Bustard pair with each week to draw hearts to attention to life with God in our every circumstance.

PARK END BOOKS